SUPERNATURAL
BUSINESS

A Better Plan

MIKE ROVNER

You ARE
SupeRNATural

Mike Rovner

Supernatural Business
© 2020 by Mike Rovner

Published by Insight International, Inc.
contact@freshword.com
www.freshword.com
918-493-1718

Unless otherwise noted, all Scriptures are taken from *Holy Bible, New International Version*®, NIV® Copyright ©1973, 1978, 1984, 2011 by Biblica, Inc.® Used by permission. All rights reserved worldwide.

Scripture quotations marked NLT are taken from the *Holy Bible, New Living Translation,* © 1996, 2004. Used by permission of Tyndale House Publishers, Inc., Carol Stream, Illinois 60188. All rights reserved.

Scripture quotations marked MSG are taken from the *Message Bible,* Copyright © 1993, 1994, 1995, 1996, 2000, 2001, 2002 by Eugene H. Peterson

Scripture quotations marked AMP are taken from the *Holy Bible, Amplified Bible,* Copyright © 2015 by The Lockman Foundation, La Habra, CA 90631. All rights reserved.

Scripture quotations marked KJV are taken from the *Holy Bible,* public domain.

The Scripture quotation marked AMPC is taken from the *Amplified Bible, Classic Edition,* copyright © 1954, 1958, 1962, 1964, 1965, 1987 by the Lockman Foundation.

The Scripture quotation marked GNT is taken from the *Good News Translation,* copyright © 1992 by American Bible Society.

ISBN: 978-1-943361-61-8
E-Book ISBN: 978-1-943361-62-5

Library of Congress Control Number: 2019910995

Printed in the United States of America

Endorsements

Each of us is given a sphere of influence so that we can advance God's Kingdom. My friend, Mike Rovner, has flourished in the business arena by operating in God's ways and wisdom. He's witnessed firsthand God's miraculous provision and intervention because he's allowed himself to be an extension of the Lord's ministry here on earth. Through God's Word and personal stories, Mike will infuse you with faith so that you can powerfully occupy your sphere of influence and experience God's supernatural work in your own business and life.

John Bevere
Best-Selling Author and Minister
Co-founder, Messenger International

A growing business is an outcome of a growing leader. My friend Mike Rovner takes you on his growth journey in *Supernatural Business*. His transparency and vulnerability will capture you and keep you engaged. It will make you reflect on your own life and give you great confidence in how to live and do business supernaturally. You'll love this book so much that you will want to share it with all your leader friends. Great book!

Sam Chand
Leadership Consultant
Author of *New Thinking—New Future*

Mike Rovner is *the* leading voice both in the marketplace and in the church. His humility, character, faith, and heart for the local church are second to none. Truly, he is a king and a priest. Mike Rovner runs a successful business and functions as both pastor and elder in our church, managing all aspects with excellence. He and Janet are absolutely a model for anyone in the marketplace. From businessman to pastor, this book is for you. *Supernatural Business: A Better Plan* is sure to change your life, your business, and your local church.

Jude Fouquier
Pastor, The City Church
Ventura, CA

I believe that the Lord is placing godly business ideas and business innovators like Mike Rovner in the marketplace to show the world what is possible when a business operates on the supernatural principles found in this book. God is moving in the marketplace, and He is blessing those who make Him the center of all they do. *Supernatural Business* is a book that will take your business to the next level.

Jentezen Franklin
Senior Pastor, Free Chapel
New York Times Best-Selling Author

The stories in this book are inspiring, and the breakthrough strategies are life changing.

Bob Harrison
"Dr. Increase" ™

Supernatural Business is an inspiring read that will open your eyes to what it means to thrive in the marketplace. In it, Mike Rovner unlocks the keys to success, launching you and your business through God's wisdom.

Phil Hotsenpiller
Founder, Influence Church
President, New York Executive Coaching Group
Author of the *Passionate Lives and Leaders* series

God loves you and has a wonderful plan for your life—and business. *Supernatural Business* is a book of miracles and supernatural insights that will help your business succeed. You will learn how to build a great team, walk in unquestioned integrity, and make better financial decisions. Mike Rovner has lived every step of the lessons he shares and has dedicated this book to your supernatural success.

John Mason
Author of numerous best-selling books including
An Enemy Called Average

Mike Rovner's *Supernatural Business* is much more than a business book. Beyond Mike's outline for key value attributes to run his successful business, Mike elevates the very reason and purpose to run a business in the first place. Beyond a profit/loss statement, Mike's MRC company serves as an engine to provide opportunities and improve the lives of its employees, vendors, and clients, and contribute its skills, money, and efforts to his ministries. The nature of his learned lessons will be valuable to readers despite what stage they are in their career. Beyond business, Mike offers insightful life lessons as well. Mike's character and faith resonate through the words in his book. Having worked with Mike for several years, I can attest that Mike really "walks the talk."

Timothy O'Brien
Senior Managing Director, Legacy Partners

Mike Rovner is the real deal. The principles and amazing stories in this book are the WHAT and HOW he used to grow his business, profits, and influence. From these principles, I've witnessed his business grow tenfold since I've been privileged to coach Mike, starting in 2006. Read and apply this book's powerful principles and expect to dramatically grow!

Tim Redmond
CEO, RedmondGrowth.com

Equal in significance to the minister on the platform leading thousands to Jesus Christ is the marketplace leader who funded it. For years, I've been saying we need a million business leaders with the Kingdom mind-set, revelation, and authority that Mike Rovner carries. Not only has he weaponized his wealth for great eternal conse-quence, but he has stewarded the influence that accompanies uncom-mon success and leveraged it to restore lives and deliver tangible hope across every sphere of society. I'm so grateful his journey of faith and inspiring testimony has been documented in *Supernatural Business*.

Dominic Russo
Founder, Missions.Me and 1Nation1Day

Special Thanks

I could not have done any of this (meaning my life, my business, or this book) without my wife, Janet. When we met more than thirty-five years ago, she looked at me and saw potential. She recognized who God wanted to make me, and she started feeding me the healthy ingredients—some amazing books and other resources—that would turn that potential into reality. Because of her, I met Jesus Christ, got addicted to business, success, and leadership books, and decided that the standard way of doing business wasn't the way we would run Mike Rovner Construction.

The other person I want to single out for special thanks is my grandmother. She is one of the most generous people I've ever met. She loaned me the $3,000 that allowed me to buy my first piece of equipment, a texture spraying machine, which eventually became a tool of a multi-million dollar a year construction company.

I also want to thank . . .

My kids, Ryan and Nicole: Being your dad has been the greatest joy of my life. I am so proud of whom you've become as adults, and I think I have learned more from you than I taught.

To my pastors, Rod and Debbie: Your mentorship and training helped make me who I am today.

To my pastors, Jude and Becky: Your supernatural faith has inspired and encouraged me to do more than I thought I could.

To my mentors, Bob Harrison and Chuck Damato: You both have helped me so much along the way, mostly by the way you live your lives.

To all the MRC team, especially Dave Holland and Cam Behtash: It would not be possible for me to do what I am doing without you.

To my mom: I love you so much, and I am so proud of you!

Contents

Foreword

I can remember the night so clearly. I was sitting in a Bubba Gump Shrimp restaurant in New York City in the middle of Times Square. I had just finished speaking at a church, and my wife and I were reflecting on all the things we wanted to do at our church back home. I pastor a rather unusual church in Los Angeles called The Dream Center. We own a hospital where hundreds of homeless people wrestling with drug addictions receive free housing and encouragement in rebuilding their lives every day. It's a city of refuge for practically every type of hurt and pain you can imagine. As we were dreaming about the future, we received a call from a construction company telling us the price of the project to finish the rest of our four hundred thousand square foot hospital. The price tag was nearly thirty-eight million dollars. The news was so overwhelming that after the call I wept. I told my wife, "It's over." I felt that the dream of renovating a hospital to help the most broken people of Los Angeles would never occur. The task was devastating. We could never afford that. We were convinced that this extraordinary hospital on the Hollywood Freeway would never fulfill its purpose.

Arriving back to Los Angeles with our tails between our legs, we received a call from a man by the name of Mike Rovner. It was as if Mike had been listening to our conversation in the middle of Times Square. He proceeded to tell me that years ago he heard me speak on Christian television about taking on the radical assignment of renovating the hospital. The vision was crazy—bringing an old hospital that was flooded with debris and completely torn up back to a thriving place of social service and community transformation. The truth is, many people didn't get behind it at first because it was so reckless they didn't think it could be done. The only bidders we had were companies that jacked up the price so high that it would never happen. This is what drove Mike to give me a call.

You see, Mike is a man who believes the impossible and expects the extraordinary. Mike lives his life by the simple phrase, "Man's need is God's call for today." I told him the price of the project we were looking at, and Mike told me he would do the project for the price of the materials and even donate workers—that's it! No profit! He would help us rebuild the hospital for the simple reason that he would be restoring a place that at one time in his life could've helped him. A couple years later, the project was done, and now the second half of that building is complete. Hundreds more people are now being reinvented. Hospital floors are completely packed with homeless veterans and human trafficking victims being rescued—all because of a man who believes in giving until it hurts.

The marketplace today can change the world for God. I'm seeing a new generation of men and women like Mike emerging everywhere. They are need-hunters who spend their lives looking for ways to be generous and looking for opportunities to give until it hurts. They completely reject the premise that having more is the measure of greatness. Instead, they understand that greatness is leaving behind many bridges that connect people to a better tomorrow.

Mike is an example of working hard for a reason. He is a man who understands that the poorest man in the world is not the person without a penny but the person without a *mission*. The power to change the world is often in the hands of those with money and corporations. However, the power to change the *hearts* of people is in the hands of a group of men and woman like Mike who understand that prosperity must have an object of love on the other side. A generous person isn't just a nice person but someone who turns the tide of places like The Dream Center, and the measure of their influence lives on for generations. Think for a second about all the people who will be rehabilitated and housed for decades to come—all because of a man who was willing to stop the profit cycle in order to use his blessing of influence to help a struggling ministry find the miracle they need to keep going.

This book is a book of miracles. It will nudge, challenge, and inspire you. At its core, it's written from a man who gets up every day of his life and says, "Yes!" to purpose. Books are great, and it's wonderful to learn truth. The difference is that *this book* comes from the soul of a man who made the ultimate comeback and never forgot those who need to rise again. Open your heart and understand that you are reading something that comes from a man of total surrender and openness who walks on water every day in his faith and mission.

Pastor Matthew Barnett
New York Times Best-Selling Author
Co-founder of The Dream Center

Introduction

In 1993, Janet and I had just gotten married. I had a small drywall repair business, and she was assisting four busy hair stylists and shampooing hair. She used to stay up late some nights after I'd gone to bed, and she'd watch the church channel on television.

One night, she woke me up after I'd gone to bed. She called up, "Mike, come downstairs. I want to show you something."

I didn't want to wake up, so I called down, "I'm sleeping."

"No," she gently insisted, "I want to show you this building downtown that Matthew and Tommy Barnett just bought. It has a bunch of drywall that needs to be repaired."

She had now woken me up, so I grudgingly came down to see two pastors on the television. One was Pastor Matthew Barnett, who at the time was probably eighteen or nineteen, and the other was Pastor Tommy Barnett, a world-famous evangelist and minister. They had just bought a building in downtown Los Angeles, the old Angels of Mercy Hospital, and they were walking through it together. Let's just say it needed a lot of work.

"See," Janet told me, "it has a bunch of drywall that needs to be repaired. I think you should go down there and see if you could repair the drywall for these guys."

I told her, "I'm going back to bed."

"I really think you're supposed to help these guys," she persisted.

I didn't know how I even could if I wanted to. I had no connections, so I headed back to bed. But God was just beginning something in our lives.

Literally, everything that happened since that late-night conversation turned out to be preparation time for me. I learned a great deal about construction and business, and much of this book is about that first fifteen years and the time directly after. It's about all the things I learned that will help anybody who wants to get from A to B, and I believe it will shorten their learning curve.

Fast forward fifteen years. Janet and I had been going down to The Dream Center, which Matthew and Tommy Barnett founded at that old hospital in downtown Los Angeles for two or three years. We'd learned a lot, and now we wanted to put on an event for businesspeople.

Janet kept confessing, "We should have Matthew Barnett come speak at our event."

"I'd love to have him speak," I answered, "but we don't even know him. How would I get him to come?"

A short time after that, a friend of ours named Bob Harrison called us and said that he was speaking at Angeles Temple, The Dream Center's church. "I want you guys to come," he told us. "I'm doing a meeting with Matthew and Tommy Barnett, and I want to introduce you to them."

A short time later, Janet and I had the honor to meet Matthew and Tommy Barnett, and I ended up becoming friends with Matthew. So, of course I asked him to speak at our conference for Christian businesspeople, which we were having at the Ronald Reagan Presidential Library in Simi Valley!

He came and spoke at our event, which was very successful. And at that event, he invited people to give their lives to Jesus. Around one hundred businesspeople—individuals who had never gone to church in their lives—gave their lives to Jesus that day.

Matthew and Tommy found out that I was a contractor, and at that time they wanted to remodel The Dream Center building. They asked if I could take a look at it and give them a bid. They'd already gotten a bid for thirty-eight million dollars, but my team and I took a look at it, not even really sure if we could do the job.

After we had a good look and run the numbers, I came back to Matthew and Tommy and told them, "This isn't a thirty-eight-million-dollar job. At the very most, it's a twenty-five-million-dollar job."

They were very excited when they heard this, and they asked me to come give a presentation to their board of directors. I told them the story of how Janet had woken me up fifteen years prior and I had even begun to make the confession that I would somehow help The Dream Center.

Everything I'd learned between 1993 and 2008 prepared me to do this work at The Dream Center, and when I told the board what we could do and how much it would cost, they hired Mike Rovner Construction (MRC) to remodel the building there in downtown LA for the world famous Dream Center.

We didn't finish the job for twenty-five million. We delivered the renovated building to them for just *seventeen* million dollars, saving this nonprofit organization over twenty-one million dollars! Not only that, the work happened during the Great Recession of 2009, when there wasn't a lot of work to be had, and so I was able to keep about one hundred of my people busy for almost four years during a down economy. That job kept my company going when many others were going out of business, so it wasn't just a great benefit to Matthew and Tommy Barnett and their organization; it was also a huge benefit to us.

While we did that project, it also exposed literally hundreds of my company's vendors and subcontractors to the Gospel of Jesus Christ through The Dream Center in a very practical way.

I've spent a lifetime in business learning the keys of how God operates in the business world, and this book is the product of everything that He has taught me. This book is about changing the very atmosphere that you and your team breathe, because this is the key to transforming your life and work from something mired in the natural into something empowered by the supernatural. The secret isn't just about self-improvement, ascribing new values, or hiring future saints. It's about changing the equation from how our work benefits us to how it moves God's Kingdom forward and helps others. When we embrace this, we go from having a business—even a Christian business—to something beyond natural.

It becomes something supernatural. But it's not about the keys God has showed me; it's about the God-inspired transformation that occurs within us. That blessing comes when we let God remake us into the people He would have us be. He wants us to be supernaturally-minded people, and when we do so as business leaders, we change the atmospheres of our businesses.

Think of this book as a cheat sheet—a way to shorten your learning curve toward having a supernatural business—because it is designed to amplify the right things already within you and to highlight the change principles that you can find in your own Bible any day of the week. Nothing in here is shocking, but it will all make a difference. None of these ideas are magic bullets. This book isn't about the key principles; it's about inspiring transformation. It's not an outline for the things you can do differently, it's about following the One who remakes our best human efforts into something beyond what humans would ever come up with. The keys point the way to Him.

I can't make you change. This book won't make you change. In fact, you can't make you change. But God can, and He has urged me to point out what has been instrumental in Him changing me. Get ready to exceed the natural, because we're about to go supernatural.

CHAPTER 1

From High to Higher

I learned a lot about business from selling drugs in my youth.

The funny thing is, when I was doing and selling drugs, I don't think anybody really worried about me. I was living in Southern California, and it was simply accepted—that's who I was. I may have been sitting in the closet with a blanket around me, tripped out of my mind or coming down off a high, but nobody seemed too concerned. It was pretty much par for the course, as selling drugs was practically our family business.

The odd thing is that when I decided to follow Jesus, people started saying, "I'm really worried about Mike." They thought it was a "phase" I was going through. They were super concerned about me, like I was going to overdose on Jesus and it would be worse than overdosing on drugs.

Well, it was no phase. Jesus changed my life in every possible way, though some have taken longer to see than others. He's still working on me today, and what He has taught me made a tremendous difference in both my life and business. I think it will also transform yours.

Starting from Broken

I grew up in a broken, dysfunctional home. My family was non-practicing Jews, and I was about forty years old when I found out that the man I'd always thought was my father was not my real dad. He hadn't been in my life since I was nine, but it was still a great shock.

When I was about ten, my mother remarried, and my new stepdad was verbally abusive to my two sisters and me. I grew up with a chip on my shoulder because he was always running me down and comparing me to his biological son, so I was determined to show him he was wrong.

But my stepdad's standards were skewed; he and my two uncles were all drug dealers. It says in my bio that I've been an entrepreneur since age thirteen—and what this means is that from thirteen I sold drugs. As I mentioned earlier, it was sort of the de facto family business! My uncle would sell me some marijuana leaves for ten dollars, and a couple of friends and I would roll them into joints and sell them at the back gate of our school for a dollar each. I'd routinely make $60 from this, so it was a pretty good return on my investment, and I learned to make money at an early age.

I also had a paper route. At ten, my stepdad told me I could no longer watch the family TV, and since I loved sports so much, I marched out and got a paper route. Around thirteen, I also started mowing lawns for a landscaper, and since my stepdad didn't want my mom spending money on us, I was somewhat self-supported by fourteen or so. By sixteen, I was helping my mom pay the bills, and by seventeen I was learning drywall repair. I was becoming self-motivated and learning the art of business, which ended up being a positive experience that helped me throughout my career.

When I was seventeen, I got a job with a drywall repair guy, also named Mike, who sprayed acoustic ceilings. Honestly, he was a horrible person and a terrible businessman, but I'm super thankful for him! He gave me my first job in the construction industry.

When I started working for my first boss, he told me that if I finished part of the job while he went to buy more materials, he would pay me a little extra money. I was super excited, so I hurried to complete my part, which was getting the house prepared to be sprayed with a new acoustic (popcorn) ceiling. When he got back, he would spray the ceiling with texture, and then we'd clean it up together and get paid.

Soon after he started inspiring my hard work with these bonuses, he would be gone for part of the day, but he'd give me an extra $40 if I could mask off the entire house, spray the acoustic ceiling material, and then get everything cleaned up before he got back. I was super excited to make the extra money, so I'd hurry to mask off the house, spray the acoustic, clean up the mess, and get all the debris out into the front yard. I also would meet with the customers, hand them the invoices, and collect the checks.

Sometimes he'd leave me waiting in the front yard for hours! I'd be completely done, with all the stuff bagged up neatly and ready to go, and he'd eventually roll up and claim there was a fire on the freeway. But inside his truck were all these fast food bags. I wondered if there really was a fire or he just took a really long lunch and had left me to do all the work for him.

This went on for a while, and he taught me a great deal about what *not* to do in business. After about four months of this (I had just turned eighteen), I realized, "Hey, I could probably do this myself!"

That was the genesis of my first business. I started my first business spraying acoustic (which totally failed) when I was just nineteen, and I had no idea how much I didn't know yet about the construction industry. But partly because of all the hard work I did for my first employer, I was learning. I also worked for my uncle, Dave, a painting contractor, and from him I learned that if you do a quality job, you'll get repeat business.

I also worked for my other uncle, Rick, who had a handyman business. He is a really smart guy, who could do all kinds of different parts of construction. It was a good time for me, because I learned a lot about myself—including that I wasn't actually very good at construction! I tried really hard, but I just honestly wasn't that good.

I could watch him hang a door thirty times, but I could never get it to close right!

During this time, he hurt his hand on a table saw, and he wasn't able to work while he recovered. Since he wasn't working, neither was I. The phone was ringing, but because he was on a lot of medication, he wasn't answering the phone. So, I asked him if it was okay if I went to give some estimates and tried to do some jobs, and since he was on meds, he told me to go ahead. I gave five estimates, and I discovered that I am actually better with people than I am at construction. I was able to connect with the people and understand what they wanted done, and they really liked me. I got all five jobs!

After a couple of days, my uncle was feeling a little better. I told him I went on the estimates and landed all five jobs. He jumped up to ask, "What are you doing going on those estimates?" I told him that he'd said it was okay. "But I was on medication," he exclaimed. Then after a moment, he asked, "How did you get all five jobs? I usually only get one or two out of five."

This is where I learned what I was good at. I was much better at the estimates and the sales than the actual construction work (which makes sense, since from the early part of my career I was a drug salesman!). I started focusing on what I knew I was good at doing from that point on.

My lifestyle of working in construction and drugs lasted into my mid-twenties until I met a girl. This girl, Janet, utterly changed my life, which sounds cliché but absolutely isn't. We met when her best friend married my uncle.

The pretty story would be that the good girl met the bad boy and reformed him, but that's not quite how we got started. I met Janet because I used to sell drugs to her!

Be Careful What You Pray For

It's amazing what can change in our hearts when we're in love. While we don't recommend dating your drug dealer, that's what Janet did. She was a backslidden Christian who kept talking about getting her life right. Someday she's going to write a book, *I Took My Drug Dealer to Church*, but that's not the whole story because she also *married* me! We both needed to get our lives right; she just recognized it, while I didn't know anything different.

One day, Janet invited me to come to church with her. I was entirely in love, so I accepted. Right after the service, she dragged me up to the front of the church, and a little woman there said, "Say this prayer and repeat it after me."

I prayed, "God, come into my life. Take the things out that You want out and put the things in that You want in, in Jesus' name."

That very simple prayer changed my life.

So did the drug raid that hit my house the very next day! They weren't even looking for me; they were looking for my uncle. God had answered my prayer, but He did it very much in His way.

That night in jail, I cried out to God. I didn't know how to pray. I just poured my heart out to Him. I asked, "God, how could this happen? How could You do this? I just prayed and gave You my life!" Now, I always tell people—be careful what you pray for! Sometimes God answers our prayers in very different ways than we expect.

I'd never been to church other than the day before, and I'd never sensed God or His presence before. But that night, He spoke to me: "I did this for you. I have a new plan for your life."

That was June 1, 1992, and my life has never been the same since.

God Was Front-Loading My Life

The crazy thing is, what I do in business now isn't that different from what I did when I was dealing drugs—I buy something big, break it into pieces, and sell it for more than I paid. The principles are the same, and I joke that I learned them all from selling marijuana.

I had no idea, but years before I met Jesus, God was already preparing my life. He was already beginning to change my life, using everything I had ever been through to lead me to Him and teach me how He works.

Janet saw potential when she looked at me, and so did God. Whatever your story is, He sees it in you, too. Whether you're an established businessperson or just getting started, young or old, successful or struggling, God sees a bright future for you. In fact, He wants to tell you this: *"I know what I'm doing. I have it all planned out—plans to take care of you, not abandon you, plans to give you the future you hope for"* (Jeremiah 29:11 MSG).

In this book, I'm going to share pieces of His plan for my life, that I think are practical, applicable, and helpful for anyone—in life or business. These are not magic incantations for explosive growth or ways to twist God's arm into giving you what you want. They are transformational concepts that have revolutionized me, personally, and my company, Mike Rovner Construction (MRC).

But before we start on the specific thoughts and practices that have helped me so much, we need to build a strong foundation. A building is only as secure as the foundation it's built on.

The foundation of your life and your business must be in knowing God. I don't mean knowing facts *about* Him—I mean getting to know Him personally. When we build on the solid foundation of a relationship with God, the specific building materials He uses to construct our lives may change, but *He* will never change. I am going to give you my keys—the materials He used to build my life and business—but the way He applies these principles in your life will be unique for you.

So, how do we get to know God?

In short, the key to building an unshakable foundation starts with prayer.

Learning How to Pray

What exactly is prayer? Some people think it's saying fancy words and using Shakespearian English, but really prayer is just talking to God. It doesn't have to be fancy, and it doesn't have to sound a particular way. All prayer needs to accomplish is talking to God.

As a young Christian, I started learning how to pray from my first pastor. He was really, really good at praying out loud. I remember listening to him and being amazed that he could do that . . . and then he asked *me* to pray! I was afraid to pray out loud, but I was embarrassed not to do it, since he'd asked me to. So, I started praying out loud, and I just tried to pray the same way he prayed. That was the start of a new life habit—praying out loud.

My pastor always ended his prayers by saying, "in Jesus' name," because Jesus left us the right to use His name. But I remember my pastor also always giving thanks to God *before* he started praying. I now understand how important this is, and he helped me form this habit early on.

Jesus serves as our example; when He prayed, He always gave thanks before He asked God to do something. As a young Christian, I started emulating my pastor and beginning my prayers with thanks. He encouraged me to pray specifically for what I was asking God to do. This is such a powerful principle for supernatural business—you must ask God for what you really want Him to do, and then believe that He answers prayer!

The best way to learn to pray is very simple: *practice*. It doesn't happen on its own; you learn through practice. Amazing things will happen when you pray for your business and for those around you.

I feel like God called me to equip, resource, and add value to the people of the workforce so they can effectively take their faith into their everyday lives and businesses. We called it a ministry to the marketplace, and its goal is to build the faith and vision of business-people by encouraging men and women toward true success and biblical prosperity, which is for building the Kingdom of God. Supernatural business emphasizes character, godliness, and strong families while training individuals to represent Jesus well and pray for people in their spheres of influence.

We've seen powerful results as people pray for their businesses, out loud, saying specifically and exactly what they're believing God to do. So, what are you asking God to do in your business?

What Is a Supernatural Business?

I want to make something quite clear from the beginning: in business, I've operated in the natural, and I've operated in the supernatural. (Selling drugs obviously falls into the "natural" category.)

I promise you, the supernatural is better! It's a better way to live your life, and it is a better way to operate your business. God was preparing me for business from an early age, and when I turned my life over to Him, He began shifting me from a natural way of doing business to a supernatural one that serves Him and others. It was only after I had a solid foundation in Him, with my life turned over to Him to do His will, that He began to grow my business supernaturally.

When I use the term "supernatural business," many people don't know what I mean at first. To them, it sounds like an oxymoron—after all, you can't mix the supernatural presence of God with the gritty, dirty truths of the secular business world. Right?

Nothing could be further from the truth!

When you operate your business in the natural, you have to work extra hard to make a profit out of every possible angle. You have to outsmart the competition. You have to work harder, longer, and craftier than everyone else so you can get recognized and get ahead. In the natural, you must depend on yourself.

But in supernatural business, you depend on God. It's not that you don't work hard; it's that you're not reliant on yourself and your abilities for your ultimate success. You rely on God. As we pray, God often shows us or tells us what to do. And when you give your business to God, you plug into His economy, which never has downturns, is never in the red, and is always life-giving!

A Supernatural Business Relies on Prayer

Some years ago, some people came to my office and offered to pray for my business. I thought that sounded great, so I invited them in. After they had prayed, one of them told me, "God wants to do something supernatural in your business, but to do that you need to get a prayer team to push you forward into the things God wants you to do."

Those words stuck with me for days afterward—a sign I have come to recognize when something said to me is God trying to get through to me. It really resonated within me, and I kept hearing those words over and over again in my head, especially in quiet times when I was driving without the radio or getting ready to pray.

I wanted God to do something supernatural in my business, and I began to learn that the supernatural is anchored in prayer. The only problem was, we often *say* that we pray, but all too often we have not truly learned to rely on God through prayer.

I witnessed this personally when I went on a mission trip to the Dominican Republic, where I quickly learned the difference between first world prayers and third world prayers. First world prayers often go something like this: "Help me get a good parking place at the mall." Or, "Please let me land this deal," or, "Help me do well in these business negotiations."

In the Dominican Republic, their prayers are like this: "God, please give us enough food for today," because without God they'll go hungry. Or, "Lord, please heal my daughter," because their town has no doctor and they couldn't pay for one even if there were one nearby.

When you have no other options, you routinely rely on God in a way we wealthy Americans seldom do (check out James 1:9-10 with this thought in mind).

I came across a group on my mission trip who were the most amazing people of prayer I have ever met. They didn't have jobs, but I immediately sensed a special connection—I needed people to pray with me, and they needed income. I knew I could help provide it because of the difference in cost of living, and so I actually *hired* a full-time prayer team!

Now, before you run off to a third-world country and try to hire a prayer team, understand this was merely the path God had for me. It's not for everyone; in fact, it may be an outlier and very unusual. But it's one way God helped bring supernaturally-minded people into the daily operations of my business. I also have people in the States who pray, because I firmly believe in the power of prayer!

I remember that in 2009 the economy had crashed, and there were a lot fewer jobs. A job became available to us, remodeling a high-rise condominium, and we vigorously bid for the project. I sent out a request to our prayer team, asking them to pray that we would get this job. Well, the building owner called me and told me that we came in second and that they thought they were going to give the job to someone else.

When the people on our prayer team asked how it was going, I told them it appeared that we were not going to get the project. And they responded back, "We still believe you are going to get the job!"

I was walking my dog and praying, "God, how are we going to get this job if they've already decided to give it to someone else?" I really felt like God wanted me to get the owner's representative out to one of our other job sites. I immediately pulled my phone out, called him, and invited him to visit one of our sites. In fact, I can't believe I said this, but I told him, "I actually insist that you come out and look at one of our jobs before you make your decision."

He could easily have said no, but somewhat to my surprise he agreed to come out and look at one of our sites. He told me that he'd be out near one of our sites on Tuesday, so we arranged for him to visit that Tuesday. I called my guys and told them to clean the site up for the visit on Tuesday.

But instead of coming out on Tuesday, he actually visited on *Monday*! We hadn't had time to clean everything up and get ready, but the owner's representative called me the next day and told me he wanted to meet.

When we got together, he told me, "I've never been to a site that was more organized and well run, where the supervisors knew the answers to every one of my questions." He was so impressed, he changed his mind and decided to give us the job! It was one of the biggest projects we'd done to that date, and it ended up carrying our company through the bad economy.

Understand this: Having a supernatural business starts with personal and group prayer. You can start by just asking friends and family to pray with you and for you and your business. The key is not geography; it's passion! (See James 5:16.)

In Matthew 18:19-20, Jesus promises us this: *"When two of you get together on anything at all on earth and make a prayer of it, my*

Father in heaven goes into action. And when two or three of you are together because of me, you can be sure that I'll be there" (MSG). That's a compelling promise!

God began to demonstrate this to me. After about ten years of working with my Dominican Republic prayer team and others, I had the thought to look back through my prayer request emails and the emails I'd sent when God answered those prayers. Because I'm one of those guys with ten billion emails in a single inbox, I just referenced them . . . and was utterly humbled and awed by all that God had done.

I have sent hundreds of emails with prayer requests, and there was not one prayer that God did not answer with something supernatural and miraculous. God answered every single one of those prayers—not always the way I'd want or anticipate, but He answered them in His timing and in His way.

No one can tell me God does not answer our prayers; I've seen Him come through too many times.

So, for those who still aren't convinced God answers prayer and still performs miracles, it makes me wonder: Are you asking? How are your motives? And if you are asking and have right motives, do you know what to ask for? These are some of the issues God brought up in my life (take a look at James 4:1-10).

I know God answers prayer; I am utterly convinced of both His love and His power. I have seen it at work in my own life when He has moved through me in ways for which I can take no credit.

If you want to see your prayers answered and the impossible come to pass, there is only one thing to do: You need to spend time with Jesus through prayer.

Spending Time with Jesus Makes You Look Smart

It's important to note that we get people to pray *with us*, not in place of us. Their prayers are not a substitute for us praying. No one can spend time with Jesus *for you*, because what we're after isn't results. It's a relationship.

A powerful preacher once told me that he spent thirty hours in preparation each time before he spoke. I wanted to improve my speaking, so I decided to emulate him, but not just for my speaking opportunities—my attempts to speak needed all the help they could get. I started putting in the same time commitment of prayer, reading the Bible, and worshiping . . . for my business.

There is no substitute for you spending time with Jesus. I began to notice that as I spent more and more time with Him, my business was more successful. As I dedicated my time to Him, I began to sign the most significant contracts my company ever had. I believe it was the result of taking on attributes of God, such as wisdom, which I was learning by spending time with Him.

Through these extended times with Jesus, God began dealing with me on topics like integrity, humility, service, courage, perseverance, honor, unity, wisdom, obedience, and more, (which we will cover in this book). He solved tremendous problems in my business—things I would've thought were impossible—and He often did so by giving me the insight, understanding, and wisdom to make strategic and ethical decisions. I could hear information and know when it was true or false, and there was no explanation for how I had this insight other than God.

When you spend time with Jesus, it will make you look smart.

I remember one time I was negotiating with a major developer—a very savvy, old-time developer. I was going to install windows on his apartment building, and he told me, "I'm going to give you this contract, but I want you to do it for $675,000." I had bid it at $750,000, so this was a big difference.

I needed this contract, but I wasn't comfortable with that kind of discount. I had prayed before this meeting, and I now felt God within me tell me that this man wasn't concerned with the price, only the quality.

I told this developer, "I am going to make sure every window in this building does not leak, guaranteed. All I ask is that you pay me the full amount."

"You'll guarantee that they won't leak?" he asked. (At the time I didn't know that the last contractor who had done windows had done a poor job and they all leaked.) He then told me, "I'll give you full price if you guarantee they won't leak!"

I did, we shook hands, and we did an excellent job on his apartments. I made sure the windows did not leak.

People began to think I was this expert negotiator, but it wasn't me—it was that I had spent time with Jesus. Peter and John in Acts 4:13 had people take note that they had been with Jesus.

Paul tells Timothy, *"Physical exercise has some value, but spiritual exercise is valuable in every way, because it promises life both for the present and for the future"* (1 Timothy 4:8 GNT). Time spent with God is never wasted, and it never goes out of style. When you spend time with God, you are investing wisely for a supernatural return. Prayer connects you with God, and when you join with God in the supernatural, you can bring it back into your natural and change that environment.

Double Double

When Janet and I got born again, we began looking for a local church. We held hands and prayed that God would send us to the church He wanted us to go to. We visited a few until in August of 1992 we found New Beginnings Christian Fellowship in Simi Valley. It immediately felt like we were in the right place at the right time. New Beginnings' focus was on new Christians, which was just perfect for me because I'd never spent much time in church. They put everything in the simplest terms possible, and from those fundamental teachings from the Bible, we learned to put into practice on Monday at our jobs what they'd taught us on Sunday.

Janet and I were completely committed to not only the truths of the Bible we were learning, but also to New Beginnings and the pastors there. As a brand-new Christian just learning to understand how God speaks, God's voice wasn't audible; it was an impression we experienced in our hearts. I felt God was urging me to stand by our pastor on several occasions and to follow what God was teaching us through our local church. That played an important and significant part of us stepping into supernatural business, and it was here that God began to truly bless us.

In 1994, a major earthquake rocked our part of Southern California. At our church, our pastor's office was damaged, and I felt like I was supposed to help. My wife and I believe in the biblical principle of returning the first 10 percent of our income to God, which in church they call a tithe. This was the first time we gave above and beyond that first 10 percent. It felt amazing to be able to give back to those who were helping us learn who God was and the value of the local church.

But something odd happened after. That year, my business started to grow, and by the next year, my company's size had doubled!

Two years later, they decided they wanted to remodel the church. Again, we felt that we were to help, so we did with our own money. I did the stucco on the outside and painted the whole church. I was so happy! God had given us another opportunity to give.

Guess what happened the next year? My business doubled again!

A few years later, the church bought an auxiliary building, and again I was able to help. I remodeled it, saving the church $100,000!

Guess what? My business doubled again!

A few years later, the church wanted to build a brand-new sanctuary building, and while I'd never done that before, I thought we could do it. It was hard, but we were able to save the church $750,000!

Can you guess what happened? That year, my business tripled!

This kind of thing just kept happening. We continued to have opportunities to do things God's way, and as we did, He blessed us over and over. God was working on me in all kinds of categories, starting with integrity, and progressively He began to trust me with more and more responsibility and influence.

I already told you about the meeting I had with Matthew and Tommy Barnett and that we saved The Dream Center twenty-one million dollars! That year, my business doubled again.

In 2 Chronicles chapter 1, God tells Solomon to ask Him for anything, and Solomon says, "Give me wisdom so I may lead Your people." The first thing Solomon does after God gives him wisdom is to build the temple, which we see in chapter 2.

In Luke 5, Peter the fisherman, having fished all night, hasn't caught a thing. Jesus tells him where the fish are, and he goes back out. After fishing all night and not being able to catch a thing, Peter has the biggest catch of his life. His catch is so big it fills his nets to the breaking point and fills his partners' nets until their boats are about to sink!

We find out in the first part of Luke 5 why Jesus did this for Peter: Jesus had been preaching and the people were pushing up against Him. He got into Peter's boat and asked him if He could use his boat so He could preach. Peter let Jesus use his boat to preach from, and then Jesus gave him the biggest catch of his life. The catch was so big, it also filled his partners' boats.

In Luke 7, Jesus heals the Roman centurion's servant. I asked myself why Jesus did this for a Roman centurion (when Jews typically didn't interact with Romans). Why did He stop what He was doing for a Roman soldier? When the Jewish leaders come to Jesus and ask Him to heal the centurion's servant, the Jewish leaders tell Jesus that the Roman centurion is a good man who built our synagogue. Hearing that, Jesus stopped and healed the Roman centurion's servant.

All of the times we gave sacrificially, God blessed us so much we were able to give to our church or to build up a local church organization or ministry. We believe that is the way that we serve the church and facilitated the growth that was part of God's plan for us and for them.

God was providing far above and beyond all I could ask or imagine. When we spend time with God, we come away looking more like Him.

If you want your business to be a supernatural business, it is vital that you spend time with Jesus and then begin to do things His way. There is no substitute for it, and there's absolutely nothing like it!

A few years after my business tripled, the church in the Dominican Republic was expanding, and Janet and I felt like God was urging us to buy the building for them. We thought we'd get some donors together and buy it as a group effort, but one person gave about $10,000, and that was about it. Janet and I still felt God urging us to buy the building, so we had to mortgage properties to buy it. But we responded and did it.

Today, ten churches have grown out of that, and "our church" is the largest in the area! We've calculated that our church has influenced the lives of Christians throughout the Dominican Republic in some way!

I don't share any of these to brag—the blessings we've experienced were not the result of something for which we can take credit. But when we did what God showed us to do, He had the opportunity to bless us—and many others. He blessed us so that we could, in turn, help others.

The year after we helped the church in the Dominican Republic, my business doubled *again*. And I didn't miss the money that came out when we responded to God's instructions and bought the church!

Through good and bad economies, God has caused my business to flourish. It isn't the result of my superior business skills, negotiating ability, hiring savvy, or leadership prowess. It's all because we decided that natural principles would not govern our business but instead supernatural ones.

I believe there are promises in the Bible and principles He has taught us for a reason—because they provide opportunities to bless us. When we apply these things to personal life change, God blesses us with a supernatural, abundant life. When we apply them to our business, we invite God to make our company a supernatural business, from which He gets the credit, and we and others get blessings.

We're going to be looking at certain principles and keys that God has taught me, but let me emphasize that a supernatural business is not just about doing the right things. It's about knowing the right Person—God.

It's not enough to merely know about Him and His ways. You can know "about" someone by reading about them, but you don't really know that person until you spend time with them. We want to know God personally, because when we do, we cannot help but be changed as we spend time with Him.

And as we begin to know Him better, we are transformed from natural businesspeople to supernatural businesspeople. Now is the best time to bring God into your business; it's time for it to become a supernatural business.

Get ready for the greatest adventure of your life!

CHAPTER 2

Someone Is Always Watching

Not to creep you out, but someone is always watching.

I'm not talking about Big Brother looking over your shoulder through an unsanctioned NSA spy program. I'm talking about the people around you. Whether you realize it or not, the people around you—Christians or not—are always watching people who claim to be a Christian. Sometimes they're just curious, and sometimes they're bitter and want to see you crash, but often they're wondering how we are going to handle the tough situations of life that come.

Mike Rovner Construction (MRC) once lost a wonderful team member who'd been with us for years, and I could tell that everyone carefully watched my reaction to their resignation, for a couple of reasons. First, we had known that another key employee would be taking an extended leave soon, and the last time they'd been gone, it had left us overexposed as a company. I'd thought we were covered, but then this other team member showed up in my office and told me they were resigning and the painful circumstances around their situation.

The second reason I knew they were all watching was the timing. This employee had just received their bonus, and they had also run up *all* of their yearly executive fund (a benefit I give to my executives, which they can access throughout the year) just three months into the year.

I could feel the eyes of everyone in the office watching how I would handle the situation. It was less than ideal—in fact, this was precisely the kind of overexposure we wanted to avoid. Now we'd be without both of them.

Let's just say I was upset when I first found out. I was a bit angry because this obviously wasn't a complete surprise—this employee had likely known trouble was coming, and if they'd said something, we could potentially have taken steps. Also, I felt kind of used; they'd waited to get their bonus, and they'd burned through all their annual spending account in just three months.

But then God began to change my thinking about it. How long had they worked hard for our company? They'd put many years of their life into MRC. Their life was breaking up around them. This stalwart, dependable employee—who was the one who'd always watched everyone else's spending like a hawk—was obviously hurting and likely not thinking super clearly.

Were they just an asset to me? Did I only value them when they were helping me make money and run my company? Or did I ascribe worth and value to them even when they were no longer contributing to my bottom line?

I felt like God reminded me that I'd made a brand out of giving people a chance to redeem themselves. After all, that's what He'd done with me, a former addict/dealer. He reminded me that He'd called me to be generous—in fact, overly generous—and that was between me and Him, not me and my employee.

God had raised me to a position of responsibility and authority, and it was *not* so that I could "spank" people when they messed up. That is not what He'd done with me, so that was not what I would do.

I realized that if this valued team member had come to me under different circumstances and told me of their problems, I would send them off with a great deal of love and thanks—and likely a nice check. So, when we sat down for their exit interview, and they told me that they hadn't intended to rack up those charges on their account, I decided not just to let the overcharge pass but to send them off with a check for five thousand extra. I wanted to thank them and to bless them. I didn't want to handle this situation like a businessman who only understood the natural order of business.

God wanted me to handle this situation like it was something supernatural.

When I gave them the check and told them how much I appreciated them, they broke down in tears. It wasn't what they expected. In the natural, they'd made things harder on us with their timing. In the natural, they'd spent more money than they should've, and they knew it. In the natural, as their boss, I should've been upset.

But in the *supernatural*, it was an opportunity to show them that their value went far beyond the contributions they made to our company.

We're Loved for Who We Are, Not What We Do

I knew the eyes of the office had watched my progression from being upset to wanting to bless my employee. They saw me take the hit and realize how it would likely affect our business, and then move through the natural, temporary discomfort. God coached me through demonstrating the different atmosphere at MRC firsthand, which instead of being based on valuing our employees for what they do, was about loving them for who they *are*. I'd like to say that I had created that culture and was doing what came naturally, but in fact, God had created this culture at MRC, and I had to get on board as much as anyone.

I guarantee that right now the eyes of those you work with are on you. They're watching to see how you'll handle that unexpected rough hiccup in your business. They see how you spend your money— and the company's money. They're checking out how you treat your spouse and family, and they're curious if you're the same person in your off hours as you claim to be on Sunday morning.

I tell you this story because a straightforward definition of integrity you may have heard is this: Integrity is being the same person in secret as you are in public. *Integrity is how you behave when you think no one is watching.*

The thing is, whether you know it or not, *they're always watching.* And if by some chance, you are alone and no one else sees, God does. He's not judging you, but He is urging you on and rooting for you to choose life (see Deuteronomy 30:19).

I cannot think of a more important concept that produces more change in a Christian than living with integrity.

It Begins and Ends with Integrity

Operating in supernatural business doesn't just happen overnight. You don't just read a book, absorb a few fundamental principles, and snap your fingers. God taught me about integrity over the course of many years—decades, really—and while I want to shorten your learning curve, I can't just hand you the nugget of how vital integrity is and expect that it will transform your life.

Only God changes lives, and for me, it all starts with integrity. Integrity now permeates everything I do—not because I've worked to make it so, but because God has baked it in as one of the critical ingredients of my changed life.

Integrity was the first supernatural business principle God began to teach me when I was doing five-hundred-dollar drywall jobs. I said, "God, I promise I will give You the credit. I'll give You the honor. I'll give You the praise for my company." That was my true prayer in the early 1990's as God was dealing with me on how I lived my life and ran my business, so He started teaching me what it would take for me to succeed.

Stay Away from the Line

As God began to teach me about my integrity, I began to realize that many people live and do business trying to flirt with an invisible line between what is legal and what is illegal, what they can get by with and what they can't. If they're especially "good," they might question what is ethical or unethical, and they may try to stay *mostly* on the right side of that line.

In the early and mid 1990's, God started to show me that He didn't even want me *near* the line. It wasn't that He wanted me to stay on the right side of it; He also didn't want me getting *close* to it, let alone flirting with it.

See, we think that we can squeeze just a little bit more profit by flirting with that line between legal and ethical vs. illegal and unethical, and on the surface that can appear right. You might save a little money cutting a corner. You might make a bit more by over-promising and under-delivering, and so forth. In the short run, it can look like you're coming out ahead, and many think that the art of this dance is the secret to being a successful businessperson.

Proverbs puts it like this: "*Make it to the top by lying and cheating; get paid with smoke and a promotion—to death!*" (Proverbs 21:6 MSG).

But God was showing me that the line wasn't just a line—it was an electric fence. People try to balance on it, but they don't understand that if they touch the fence, they're going to get a shocking surprise. They're going to get burned, and when they do, they'll burn the people (such as their employees and clients) around them. No one falls off on the right side when they walk on the electric fence; they always fall on the wrong side, and if they flirt with disaster long enough, eventually they *always* get burned.

I remember before I became a Christian, I once went to the building supply store (it was actually named Home Base) and saw that bags of acoustic for spraying ceilings were mispriced. They were supposed to be $6 or $7 a bag, and they had them marked about $2 a bag. It wasn't a sale; it was a mistake.

So, I asked them how many bags they had, and they said that they had two hundred bags. I knew it was the wrong price, but I liked the sound of saving money, so I bought them all. Something in me, even before I knew God, understood that wasn't right. But I wanted to get ahead, so I cheated the store and bought the bags despite that inner misgiving.

When I was over halfway through the bags, some moisture got into my garage where I was storing them and ruined those remaining bags of acoustic! I saved $600 by buying them at the wrong price, but I lost most of those bags, so if anything, it ended up costing me hundreds of dollars. In the short run—that day—it seemed like I'd saved money. But in the long term, I got burned.

This is what it's like when we flirt with the line; you might think you're saving money, but in the end, it's going to cost you.

I remembered that situation about buying the bags of acoustic after I started following Jesus, and God showed me that it was a teaching moment about integrity that He worked into my life even before I knew Him. It has served as an object lesson for me ever since. He was teaching me that is just the way it happens—sooner or later, when we flirt with the line, eventually we get burned.

Trust Is Currency

God began showing me that living a life of integrity had benefits that went far beyond my business's bottom line. The most significant benefit I noticed was that unlike the people who get burned and burn those around them, when you stay far away from the fence and live with integrity you can build lasting, meaningful trust. And trust is the currency of life—in life, and in business.

Trust takes a lifetime to build, but it can burn up in an instant. In business, trust can be the difference between getting a job that you've bid on or not. It can be the difference between keeping a loyal customer or losing them. It can mean keeping well-trained, loyal employees or losing them to a competitor. In life, trust can be the difference between a thriving marriage and a dying one, strong friendships or shallow ones, and healthy relationships with your kids instead of weak ones that don't survive them leaving the house.

The list goes on and on. Trust is currency!

You might think that you're saving or making money by cutting corners, trying to get by with things, and walking on the fence, but all of those gymnastic moves you need to do to stay up there will wear you out. And when you fall—not *if*, it's *when*—you will burn up any perceived gains you've made, and you will break trust. It may be with a client, it may be with employees, or it may be in your home—but once lost, trust takes a long time to regain.

God's path is different. He calls His people to live with integrity. The payoff is that you never burn up that trust you've worked hard to build, and it pays off in the end.

Do the Right Thing

Earlier I told you that one definition of integrity is how you behave when you think no one is watching. That's perhaps actually a better way to reveal your integrity than define it.

The dictionary tells us that integrity is steadfast adherence to a strict moral or ethical code, but to me, this sounds like it's more about keeping the rules than the condition of your heart. Remember, we're not talking about dry principles; we're talking about life change. So, let's look a little deeper at what integrity means.

Integrity is doing the right thing, at the right time, for the right reason. It's not just about the actions you take; it's also about when

43

you do it and why you do it. And to me, that's why integrity is important to God—because it's about your heart and motives.

I am not talking about earning God's approval here. But does God care what we do and why we do it? Is how we act important? I believe it is. Proverbs 21:3 tells us that *"Clean living before God and justice with our neighbors mean far more to God than religious performance"* (MSG). Obviously, God likes it when we do the right thing, but we are made right with God because of what Jesus did, not through anything we do on our own (check out Romans 3:22).

God loves integrity because He doesn't just want robots, merely doing the right thing because we have been programmed to do so and have no choice. I believe that God wants people who have learned who He is and have seen His character and emulate what He does.

You can look at it like this: God does not want slaves, He wants partners.

Do You Want to Make Partner?

My good friend George started with a huge company as a construction superintendent, and on his very first job, which was to take about six weeks, the owners told him they needed it done in two weeks. He told them there was no way they could get it done that soon, but the owner insisted that they needed it done in two weeks. So, George grouped his people into different crews working in three separate eight-hour shifts, twenty-four hours a day. When the two weeks were up the owner came to see how the job was going, and he couldn't believe his eyes—George had done the impossible, and the job was done.

George worked the impossible for these guys, and he was on the fast-track with them. He was a diligent, hard worker, and in time they promoted him to project manager and eventually to the senior construction manager. Because George worked so hard and treated the business like it was his own, he did very well for the owners and helped make their business successful.

One day the two partners who owned the company asked George to meet with them. During the conversation, they asked George this question: "If we were in trouble and needed you to lie for us to get out of trouble, would you do it?"

George had to think pretty carefully about his answer. If he said "yes," wanting to seem like an earnest employee willing to do whatever it took for the good of the company, it might make him look better. But George was a person of integrity. If he said "no," he considered that they might not think he was committed and loyal to the company.

Eventually, George answered them, "I would work very hard to help solve the problem. I would do whatever I could. But I would not lie for you."

"George," they replied. "If you had been willing to lie for us, we would have kept you as a senior construction manager, since you're great at your job."

George's heart sank at those words.

"But because you are not willing to lie for us, we would like to promote you to partner." Today, the partners have retired, and George is the president of this nine-figure company—and it was integrity that opened the door for him.

In the Parable of the Talents, the master tells the first two faithful servants, *"Good work! You did your job well. From now on be my partner"* (Matthew 25:21 MSG).

God wants you to live boldly and to use the gifts He's given you His way. He wants us to trust Him. In business, this means that He wants us to do it His way—even when it looks like it might cost us money. When we do, we're showing that we trust that His way works. When we do not, we are showing that we are living out of fear.

You might think you're a daring mover and shaker, but if you're not living with integrity, in reality, you're flirting with the line because you're afraid. You're scared to do it God's way, so you're doing it your way. That's pride (which we'll talk about later).

Proverbs tells us that there is a way that seems right at the time, but in the end, it leads to disaster (check out Proverbs 14:12). That's business as usual for those who live on that line between right and wrong.

But instead of following our way, we are supposed to trust God and not try to do it all on our own. We're supposed to be listening to His voice in everything we do and everywhere we go because He is the One who enables us to live with integrity (see Proverbs 3:5-6).

It's Not a Gift, It's a Test

This may surprise some people, but God does not give us opportunities to cheat or give us blessings through errors that cost others. I remember back to another Home Base moment from before I became a Christian. I put some things in a bucket that I was buying, and when I put it all on the register, I put something on top of the bucket to save space. The cashier was lazy and didn't check inside the bucket. I realized afterward that though I hadn't intended to steal the items inside the bucket, I'd gotten it for free because of their inattentiveness (and the fact that I hadn't brought it to their attention).

The first time this happened, it was an accident on my part. The next couple of times (remember, this was before I was a Christian), it wasn't so much an accident on my part as it was exploiting a flaw in their training.

A lot of people would say this is a gray area. Was it their fault for not training their people right, or was it mine for exploiting the hole in the system? However, I remember that I began feeling this sickness in my stomach. I was stealing, and even though I wasn't saved yet, God called me on it, and my conscience pricked me.

Today, God has called me to live differently. I now no longer see someone else's mistake that benefits me as a gift.

It's not a gift. It's a test.

Let's say you pay in cash at the store, and they give you too much change. Is it a gift? Or what about my Home Base buckets? Were the things inside them "gifts"? Or was I *stealing*? Now, I see them both as stealing. I no longer see it as "gray"—it's either right, or it's wrong.

God does not bless us through mistakes or by cheating, even if it's by accident. If that kind of thing happens, it's a test of your integrity.

When I was just getting started in construction, and before I started going to church, I remember one time when a client overpaid me. I thought it was bonus time, and I kept it. "Their mistake, their loss," I thought. A few years later after I was now a new Christian, I got overpaid again. Guess what I did? I still kept it! But I sent them a note and said, "You overpaid me; on your next invoice I'll give you a credit." God was just starting to work on me, and at least I was making progress!

I'm not saying that we're perfect on these kinds of tests (by the way, God isn't asking you for perfection). But my wife and I have developed a strong belief that these mistakes in life, which some people treat like blessings, are in fact character tests. We're busy people, and we've felt inspired to drive five or ten miles through LA traffic to make even a small mistake right. Today, if someone overpays the company (and that happens a lot), there's a reimbursement check out to them immediately for the difference, which is now sometimes a great deal of money.

You might be thinking, "It's not worth it to take all that time to return it when it's just a few bucks." In a way, you're right—my time is valuable, worth way more than the paltry few dollars from the error. But something else is even more valuable to me.

Let me ask you this: How much is your integrity worth to you? How much would you *pay* to *buy* a reputation for trust and honesty? Your reputation is worth a lot in business—remember, trust is currency. Proverbs 22:1 says, *"A sterling reputation is better than striking it rich . . . "* (MSG).

So how much would you sell your integrity for? Would you sell it for thousands of dollars? Millions? How much does it take before you do the right thing and inconvenience yourself for the sake of your integrity?

How would you feel if I told you that some of us are willing to sell our integrity for pocket change? The thing is, God does not work on a sliding scale. It's "not okay" when the amounts are small and "not okay" when the amounts are substantial.

God started with me on the little things. He taught me to be faithful in those small things. And then, gradually, He tried me with bigger ones. It reminds me of a scripture. Jesus tells His disciples, *"If you're honest in small things, you'll be honest in big things"* (Luke 16:10 MSG). The converse is right, too—if you're dishonest with little things, you'll be dishonest with big ones.

See, we think that we can let the little things slide and then when it "really matters," we'll do the right thing. But we don't realize that all the little things are setting a precedent.

Right now, God is looking for people who will be faithful with earthly wealth, because it's training for how to handle heavenly blessing. He wants people who will show integrity with the little things so that He can entrust us with more significant things.

Jesus goes on just a few verses after the scripture above to say, *"No one can serve two masters. For you will hate one and love the other; you will be devoted to one and despise the other. You cannot serve God and be enslaved to money"* (Luke 16:13 NLT).

In Luke's version of Jesus' story of the servants who invested their master's money, upon his return, the master tells the first servant, *"Good servant! Great work! Because you've been trustworthy in this small job, I'm making you governor of ten towns"* (Luke 19:17 MSG).

How you use what God has given you—whether you invest your time, energy, money, and talent with integrity or not—determines what He does next. He can either give you more significant responsibilities and blessings . . . or He can give you the same test again.

I want to emphasize that I'm far from perfect, and again, God isn't after our perfection—He's after our hearts. Is your heart following after God? He wants you to pass! He wants to give you more. But He won't do it until you're ready.

Mistakes Happen

I certainly haven't always gotten it right. Years ago, this lady did the flowers when Janet and I got married. She said that instead of paying her the $300, she'd like me to do some drywall work for her. Well, the problem was that in the middle of all this, her live-in boyfriend ended up owing me about $6,000, and I decided that I was never going to work with him again.

I ended up never doing the drywall at the florist's house because of her boyfriend, and I completely forgot about it. Well, years later I felt like God reminded me about it, and I felt like I needed to pay her the $300.

I figured since I was a Christian now that I'd pray about it. I wanted to set the record straight with God, so as I prayed I reminded Him that the boyfriend never paid me my $6,000 and I was being generous by just "calling it even." But as God kept dealing with me on it—a process we call "conviction"—I kept feeling like I was supposed to pay her.

And wouldn't you know it, one day I saw them in Costco! No sooner did I lay eyes on them than I felt like I was supposed to write them a check for the $300! I happened to have a check in my wallet, and I immediately got it out and wrote them a check for the money we owed her. I went over to them, and I gave it to her. They thanked me and were very surprised I remembered.

I am very much still growing in integrity, and I will tell you this— you are not alone and responsible for increasing your integrity. If you are a Christian, you have God living inside you. He has the power to change your life, and He will teach you how to live with integrity.

CHAPTER 3:

The Benefits of Integrity

In the previous chapter, I mentioned that no one ever falls on the right side of the fence. Sooner or later, you're going to get burned, and when you fall, it's always on the wrong side. That's just a natural consequence—it's not a punishment, it's just what happens.

However, the converse is also true: There are many benefits to operating in integrity. We all know that if you're trying to get someone to buy into something, you talk about the benefits. Let's examine some of the many benefits God has shown me—things such as healthy relationships, financial well-being, and long-term success (all of which we've already talked about a little). However, four benefits stand out to me to explore in this chapter: protection, influence, joy, and favor. Let's start by taking a look at how integrity protects us.

Integrity Protects You

Many people think that God's ways of doing things ruin their fun—they believe that God is grumpy and stern and doesn't like us to enjoy ourselves.

Nothing could be further from the truth.

The truth is, God's way is for our protection. He is a God of natural consequences—He created a universe where if you drop a raw egg on the floor, it breaks. It's not evil that eggs break when you drop them; it's just a natural consequence of falling from your hand.

My daughter didn't like having a curfew, but as her father, I knew that the risk of severe accidents and violent crimes went up dramatically after midnight. I wasn't trying to steal her fun; I was trying to protect her by telling her to be home by midnight.

When God gives us instructions about living with integrity, it's like a seatbelt. Seatbelts save lives. Some people don't like wearing them and think that seatbelts restrict their freedom. But the reality is that if you're ever in a car wreck, you want to be wearing your seatbelt. Proverbs 13:6 tells us, *"Righteousness guards the person of integrity, but wickedness overthrows the sinner."*

Years ago, I was audited by the EDD—the State of California Employment Development Department. And let me say, this is a bad deal, and these guys are way worse than an IRS audit. The EDD plays for keeps!

After the audit, the EDD handed me a bill for $80,000. I had to hire an accountant for $100 an hour to start getting things straightened out. He informed me that we had been making some mistakes. Because we had made these mistakes, it was going to cost us. Now, I honestly did not know at the time that I was doing the wrong thing, but had I known the right thing to do from the beginning, it could've saved me a lot of money. Had I known the guidelines, they could have protected me.

God gives us His guidelines, and if we follow them, they protect us.

The thing is, God had started working on me to live life with integrity years before the EDD audit. I could have hired an accountant earlier to make sure I was doing things the right way, and it probably would've saved me a lot of pain (and money).

God is not trying to keep you from something good by calling you to live a life of integrity. He's trying to protect you. Remember, He guards us when we walk in integrity.

What is God trying to guard in your life? He wants to safeguard your business, your marriage, your finances, and much more—your whole life! When you're a Christian, God also wants to guard your reputation so you represent Him well to others—what we call your "testimony."

In 1 Timothy 4:16 Paul tells young Timothy, *"Keep a firm grasp on both your character and your teaching. Don't be diverted. Just keep at it. Both you and those who hear you will experience salvation"* (MSG).

Integrity Gives You Influence

God wants to give you influence, and that is the next benefit of integrity I want to show you. At the start of the previous chapter, I told you that someone is always watching. The truth is that because we're being viewed, people of integrity have a tremendous opportunity for influence.

I remember working as a drywall repair guy for this tough-nosed individual who owned a body shop. He was a good businessman in certain ways, but he only knew the natural way of doing business. I was busy learning the supernatural way of doing business, and it caused us to cross each other a few times. And while he was a tough-nosed guy, I'm pretty stubborn (I mean "persistent")—especially when it's something I believe in passionately. And because I was learning these godly supernatural business principles, I was very "passionate" in some of our conversations.

At the time, it just seemed like a cause of friction; I knew things should be done God's way, and he was used to doing them the way most people do them because he thought it would make or save him money. But here's the thing—while it was a cause of friction at the time, I didn't understand these arguments were also opportunities to influence him.

Years later he began to date a woman who was a Christian, and a few years later they got married. One day he called me and said, "Mike, I just wanted to let you know that I accepted Jesus Christ as my Lord and Savior." He later told me that the way I'd dealt with him was going through his mind when he made his decision to accept Jesus. He remembered things I'd said and principles I'd tried to stand up for, and he now understood that they'd influenced him.

As my responsibility and authority have grown, so too has my influence. Today, I see it as a core part of what I do—representing God in the marketplace. We think that only belongs in Sunday services, on mission trips, or with some evangelist on TV, but I firmly believe that our everyday lives are the best place for influencing others and showing them the power of what we believe.

When you live a life of integrity, you allow God to influence others through you.

Integrity Protects Your Joy

Think about it—when you have a secret, you're always concerned that secret could get uncovered. If you're keeping secrets at work (areas where you've cheated or compromised), somewhere in the back of your head, you're anxious that someday you could be exposed. The same is true at home—if you're keeping things from your spouse, is your relationship as open and transparent as it could be? Of course not. And what if they find out someday? Will it cost you your marriage? These kinds of concerns are at the root of much of our stress.

Secrets rob you of joy.

The opposite is also true. There's a kind of joy that comes from God when you're living His way that goes beyond happiness. Psalm 119:1 tells us, *"Joyful are people of integrity, who follow the instructions of the Lord"* (NLT). Why are they joyful? Because they're not nervous about skeletons falling out of their closet!

Earlier I told you that one of my favorite definitions for integrity is doing the right thing at the right time for the right reason. When you know what you're supposed to do and do not do it, it produces stress. You are anxious because you know you're doing the wrong thing, or you're not doing it when you're supposed to, or you're doing it with the wrong attitude or motives. However, when we do it God's way, none of those problems follow you—you're free to enjoy your time, because you did what you needed to do when you needed to do it.

At the end of 1999, the first big year Janet and I had ever had, we met with our accountant, and he said that we owed a certain amount in taxes. So we paid our taxes right at the start of 2000, and in February he met with us again and said, "We made a mistake. You owe more taxes."

I asked, "How did 'we' make a mistake? I'm a contractor, and you're a tax professional."

He told me, "You owe $100,000 more than I told you." But then he said, "But don't worry, we can cook the books, and you won't have to pay it. And if you get caught, you probably won't go to jail."

The first thing I said was, "You are *so* fired!" And second, I told him, "We'll pay our taxes." Remember, Jesus told us, "*Give back to Caesar what is Caesar's and to God what is God's*" (Mark 12:17). But we didn't have the money, so we thought we'd just have to make payments.

At the beginning of April, we got a phone call from someone that we work with. We'd made an investment into one of his buildings, but we had no management in the building and weren't running the project. He said, "We have an all-cash offer on the building." That sounded good to me! "We're going to sell it," he went on, "and you're going to make a really big profit."

I replied, "That's great! I can use it to pay toward my taxes. How much am I going to get?"

He told me, "You're not going to believe this, but you're going to get $99,000!"

I got that money on April 14th, and we were able to pay our taxes. It was just one way God showed me that He would do things supernaturally if I just followed His way. God is the author of joy. His joy is our strength, and because of Him I had the strength to not cook the books. He helped me preserve my integrity, and with it His joy in my life.

The Favor of God

God does not accept or love us because of what we do. The Bible teaches that we are in right standing with God thanks to Christ Jesus. Let's get that out of the way.

That said, what we do matters. We can position ourselves for excelling, or we can position ourselves for hardship. Integrity will open doors for you that reflect God's favor—His unmerited approval—on your life. I'm not saying we earn His goodness; I'm saying that when we position ourselves through lives of integrity, we are lined up correctly and can receive opportunities we would otherwise miss.

This was made real for me when we were still a very small construction company. I saw that there was a large multifamily owner doing the exact kind of work in which we specialized on their property, so I contacted them and told them I'd like to do some work for them. They told me that they didn't need me because they had someone else, but they agreed that I could contact them in the future. Every few weeks, I'd reach out to them. However, eventually the guy I was contacting got exasperated with me calling him and with having to repeatedly tell me, "We don't need you!"

So, I can take a hint, but I really believed God had this for me—I started faxing them instead! And it just so happened that one day when the developer and the senior vice president were talking about what they were going to do because of a problem with their contractor, they saw my fax.

"My name is Mike Rovner, and I can help you," it said.

I ended up getting a contract for this job that was about 80 percent bigger than anything I'd ever done before—and with that bigger job came 80 percent more exposure! I felt like Peter stepping out of the boat to walk on the stormy sea with Jesus—it was a massive step of faith!

Remember "be careful what you pray for"?

Well, I'd wanted to work with this company for so long, and now I finally did! However, the owner's representative was one of the worst people to work with that I've ever encountered! He wanted us to do a level of work that was impossible for their budget, and on top of that, he was profoundly racist and abrasive. I started getting complaints from my staff and subcontractors almost immediately.

One day he and I were on a site together, and I just had to stop him and say, "Please don't speak to me that way." Now, understand, I'm in construction. I've heard it all! But this guy was absolutely the worst!

He didn't respect my request and just laughed me off, and it was becoming a big problem for the people I had on the job sites. No one wanted to work for him or be near him, and they were almost ready to walk off the job because of him.

I realized that I could either let things keep going the way they were going, and I would lose some outstanding people, or I could make his boss aware of the situation and see if they could do anything. The problem was if I shared this information and they did nothing, this guy could ruin me because I had so much invested in this project.

Earlier I told you that if we listen to God, He will always guide us into wisdom and the path of integrity. In my desperation about what to do, I realized that I had better pray. It was at least worth a shot!

I felt like God impressed on me that I needed to do what was right, no matter what the cost. That was not what I wanted to hear!

So I drafted a letter to the senior vice president of the company, and I also called the construction manager. I ended up meeting with him, but his boss didn't do anything at all. I then met with the vice president, and he didn't do anything, either. I was now *really* exposed!

However, something else happened. This vulgar construction manager had also sexually harassed women at this company, but they had not reported it because they were afraid. He'd been racist towards others, who'd also not reported him. But when they heard that I had spoken up against his behavior, it encouraged them to come forward. Without me coming forward, they never would have.

Two weeks later, the construction manager was off the job, fired.

Because of working with this one company, we got millions of dollars of referrals, not to mention the work we continued to do for them for years. We've remodeled thousands of apartment units because of our success with that job, but it would not have happened had I not stood up and done what was right.

I consider all the work we did for that company and the many, many referrals I received after doing a good job for them to be God's favor on me and MRC. Integrity (doing the right thing) opened those doors, and God poured blessings through them.

When you do what is right in tough situations, God is going to bless you. It will often not be easy; you will run great risks to obey Him.

Practical Integrity

We have talked about some of the benefits of integrity, but I have found that it's beneficial to make something practical, to make it real. So, what does it look like to live and walk with integrity?

One of the first things the Lord showed me was keeping my word. When I said something, I wanted it to be 100 percent true all the time. The Bible puts it simply: *"Don't say anything you don't mean . . . "* (Matthew 5:33 MSG).

This is very important in business, and at MRC we're really big about telling the truth—even when it's not the news a client wants to hear. Construction isn't a perfect science, and we've had to go into meetings and tell clients the truth: "Your building isn't going to be ready on time." (Most of the time, it's not our fault, but we end up with the blame whether we deserve it or not.) They don't want to hear that, but it's the truth. I would rather be known for always telling the truth than saying what I thought my clients wanted to hear when the fact is something different.

Here's old wisdom: Mean what you say and say what you mean. Tell the truth, even when it hurts.

A side note on this—some people don't tell the truth because they are afraid of conflict. They're worried that if they say the wrong thing, it could lead to conflict, so they say what they think will avoid trouble, even when it means altering the truth. But if you want to be a person who strives for integrity, you have to push back that feeling and speak the truth in love (see Ephesians 4:15). No one likes confrontation; I personally don't like confrontation. But to run a supernatural business, you have to get somewhat comfortable with confrontation or at least be able to push through conflict. You need to be able to bring people up in love and not spank them.

I was recently in the car with someone when we got a phone call. We were still an hour away, but they told the person calling we'd be there in half an hour.

"Not without a rocket!" I said.

This isn't the first time something like this has come up, and it made me wonder why we, as people, say things that aren't true. Often, we just don't want people to be upset that we are not doing what we said. We don't want them to be disappointed.

Trust me, people are going to find out . . . when we're half an hour late! The truth is going to come out, whether you try to avoid conflict or disappointment or not. But when we tell these "little white lies," people are not only going to be disappointed, they're also going to be upset that we told them something that wasn't true on top of it.

I'll tell you this: You may appear to have more conflict in the short run when you choose to tell the truth and be a person of high integrity, but in the long term you will be respected for it. Respect must be earned, and honesty and integrity will win you a great deal of respect.

People respect those who are candid—frank and honest. They appreciate consistency and being the same person no matter the situation (being the same person in public that you are in private). They'll be surprised if you're transparent, because that takes courage, especially in today's world where it is so rare.

I remember learning this with my pastor. We had pastor's council meetings on Thursday nights, and on Sunday my pastor would often ask if I'd be there Thursday. Early on, I would often tell him "Yes," even when I knew that my travel schedule might make it unlikely I could make it. I didn't want to disappoint him.

I should've said, "Pastor, I have a meeting Thursday, and I don't know if I'll be able to make it." I had to grow into that, and now I transparently share my schedule with my pastor.

Being a person of integrity will often involve saying "no" to people. It's an uncomfortable word sometimes—it's unpopular. But the word "no" is freeing, and it's honest. If you don't use that word often, you might practice it as you read right now: Say *"No!"* See, you can do it!

Being a person of integrity and transparency also means admitting your mistakes and taking responsibility. There are always going to be times where we let people down or fail at something. However, we can own up to those things, accept responsibility, and be honest. That is being a person of integrity.

I once was at a real estate conference where this guy came up to me and said, "Aren't you *that contractor*?" I wondered what he meant by that, and we quickly discovered that he knew somebody who knew somebody who knew the owner of this building we'd worked on—talk about word of mouth!

The story was this: On a Friday afternoon, a roofer had hit a waterline on some of the condominium units we were remodeling in Brentwood. It was the worst possible scenario because no one noticed—and the units flooded *all weekend*. When my crews came back Monday, it looked like someone had hit a fire hydrant because there was so much water coming out!

There were five or six inches of water inside the units. It was a disaster!

I quickly met with my people and then the owners, and then I called the insurance company. And guess what they said: "Why don't you just vacate the job?" They said they'd call appraisers and adjusters to come out; they'd get the process moving and then let the attorneys figure it out.

However, God reminded me that I'd signed a contract to be done by a specific date, and the insurance process could take years.

The roofer was out; he went with what the insurance company said. The problem was, I didn't have the resources to remodel the units again, so I talked to the owner and told him I wanted to honor the date we'd agreed to for the contract, but that we didn't have the resources. Since it was in his best interests to get the repairs done, we were able to agree that they'd take care of part and we'd take care of the other part. We took pictures for the insurance company, and then we got to work.

We completely redid the units, and it cost us every penny of the profit from that job. Being honest was the easy part; making it right was a challenge, but it was worth it.

The owner was able to sell them sooner rather than later, making a nice profit. However, the story doesn't stop there. I met with the owner again after it was all over, and I would typically expect that something like this would be a permanent black mark for us. However, he told me, "Rovner, in the worst possible scenario, you did what was right." He leaned forward. "You are the contractor for us," he said, and within six months I had jobs from them that were ten times the value of that one job!

It doesn't end there! The insurance company paid me back every dime, plus 20 percent. The roofer who walked off the job never worked with us again. However, I did work for the owners for many, many years, and it made MRC famous because of their good word of mouth. As illustrated by the guy at the real estate conference, word spread about how we'd handled that with integrity and honesty.

The Holy Umpire

Because I speak about integrity and supernatural business a great deal, people often ask me for spiritual tips on how to live with integrity, and I want to give you two more. I typically tell them that it is not about a list of "Do's" and "Don'ts." First, I tell them supernatural integrity is about listening to the gentle whisper of God's voice guiding you. When you have Jesus in your heart, He can sound like your conscience, but it's actually God's Spirit living inside you. Second, I tell them that spiritual integrity is about finding people you can trust who are allowed to speak even the hard truths into your life.

I love the way the *Classic Amplified Bible* translates Colossians 3:15: "*And let the peace (soul harmony which comes) from Christ rule (act as umpire continually) in your hearts [deciding and settling with finality all questions that arise in your minds]. . . . "*

God wants to be your umpire. He wants to call "out" what is out and "safe" what is safe.

That means when you do not know what to do, you ask Him—and you expect Him to answer you. You give Him the right to veto any decision you make, and when He speaks, you obey—no arguing or complaining!

Practically, this often looks like following the peace. If you face a situation, ask God what to do in prayer. They can be simple prayers: "God, help me! Show me the way and give me wisdom." Then wait to see if you have peace. If you have peace about one decision and not the other, this is often God guiding you. I like to close my eyes and imagine going down one path or another, and then I wait on Him to see which gives me more peace.

It's uncanny how often God has told me to do the hard thing and has given me the peace I need to do it when the wrong thing would be "easier." Learn to follow His peace and let it be the Holy Umpire for your life.

A final note on this: The peace of God will never contradict anything in the Bible. While the Bible does not spell out every specific for your business, it is nevertheless a guide for life and business unlike any other! It's as relevant today as it was 2,000 years ago. Proverbs especially is full of wisdom, and you can gain a great deal of spiritual, practical, and even business insight into God's path of integrity from what God says in the Bible.

You also have to give certain people the right to speak into your life. I have very selectively asked people in my inner circle I trust implicitly to speak into my life, recognizing that they are people who hear from God. My wife is at the top of this list, but others include my pastors, my mentor, my CFO, and my senior vice president at MRC.

I have asked them to help hold me accountable, and I have given them permission, in advance, to bring up anything they may see in my life that is not according to God's standard. They can call me on it, and I have already promised to listen and respect what they have to say.

The people you can trust for this purpose of accountability are those in whom you've seen godliness and integrity over an extended period of time. They're trusted, long-term relationships that have been tested. They are people who love you (and love you sacrificially) and want the best for you.

The more successful you get, typically the more your inner circle will shrink because while many people will want influence with a successful person, few will love you and want the best for you for who you are instead of what they can get *from you*. Choose wisely.

Allowing select people to speak into your life requires being in a place of humility and, to a degree, submission to them (topics we will cover later in the book). The first time one of them brings up an issue, it will be hard—frankly, it's always hard to hear it from someone else that you've dropped the ball. However, this kind of candid, transparent relationship is one of the biggest strengths for those who live with integrity.

How You Treat Others

Other people are attracted to individuals of integrity. They will work really hard for you, and that means that you have a responsibility to them.

Several years ago, one of our superintendents was doing a side job in addition to his regular job for MRC. It was very important to me to get this work done, and the superintendent was working very hard at his regular job and then also helping out significantly after hours on a building that Janet and I had purchased.

My vice president, Dave Holland, approached me and said, "Listen, this is one of our best people. He's super committed to helping us, and you are pushing him to the limit. He may not have enough time to spend with his family because you're asking him to do so much additional work."

I remember being a little set off by that. I thought if it was too much additional work, why didn't he just tell me? But Dave helped me understand that this superintendent was so committed, he would work his fingers to the bone for us. He didn't want to disappoint me and wouldn't want to be seen as a complainer.

I don't ever want to hurt anyone, and I had to listen to what Dave was telling me because overworking this guy was hurting him. "You know, you're right," I told Dave.

People will feel passionately loyal to you when you are a supernatural businessperson of integrity. For your part, you must always ask yourself if you are doing right by them, because they will try so hard to do right by you. Integrity doesn't just mean doing what is right for you; it means doing right by others, as well, and looking out for what's best for them.

What Will You Be Known For?

Early on when we began talking about integrity, I mentioned that people are always watching. I do not want to imply that we behave with integrity to be seen by others. However, we walk with integrity because God always sees, and I for one want to know and imitate the heart of God. When we emulate Him by acting with integrity, we are living testimonies about who He is and what He is like. The benefits and influence follow as natural results.

You are going to be known for *something*. It's your choice what it is. Do you want to be known for how you're able to say just exactly what people want to hear? That you were really good at walking the fence?

Or will you be known for your integrity?

I know which one I choose.

CHAPTER 4:

Practicing Total Dependence

Several years ago, I had an incident with an employee whom I had worked with for many years—in fact, we'd been friends since we were twelve years old. I had originally hired John as a journeyman carpenter, but he had advanced within MRC to become one of my top supervisors.

Well, one day we got into a disagreement while at a job site. We began talking it over, but what started out as a disagreement about how to handle an employee turned into a heated argument. This longtime supervisor told me, "If you don't trust my judgment on this issue, then I need to quit."

I was so hot, I shot back, "If you don't respect my authority, then you will be fired!"

Didn't he realize I was *the boss*? He had to respect my authority! With this reasoning, I held my ground. Then he told me he was quitting. I told him that as far as I was concerned, he was already fired.

As you can see, this situation was degenerating quickly!

A couple of days later, my top advisor and vice president, a man I've known and respected for many years named Dave, came into my office. Now that I'd cooled down, he wanted to offer me his thoughts. (Remember, you have to give some people permission to speak honestly into your life, and he is one of those people for me.)

"You can fire him if you want," he told me, "but he is a great guy, and it is difficult to find a supervisor who executes as well as he does."

I sat back in my chair, really thinking about what he'd said. I thought about the years I had spent training and mentoring this supervisor. I was ready to fire him, allowing another company to take advantage of everything I'd invested into him.

I suddenly had a bright idea: Maybe I should ask God for guidance! "God," I prayed, "what should I do?"

After praying about it, I started to think of all the years I'd spent mentoring John. He did really well for our company, and now that he was so well trained, was I really going to fire him over a simple difference of opinions?

I suddenly knew that I needed to humble myself, reach out to him, and make a real effort to work around our differences. When I reached out to John in humility (not acting like a whipped dog, but simply more open to his point of view), he responded very positively. He replied, "I'm so sorry this happened, but I just didn't know how to say I was sorry."

We talked it through, and because I was no longer taking a "my way or the highway" approach, we were able to work it out, and he is still a good friend and an amazing employee. In fact, though I didn't know it at the time, God was working on some things in his life, which I will tell you about later.

God was teaching me then—and still is teaching me—about what it truly means to be humble. It isn't what I thought it was at first, and despite what you might assume, humility is actually an asset in business.

It's Not About You

Church circles and business circles have radically different ideas about pride and humility. In business, the word *pride* is just feeling good about yourself and the work you do; it's like self-esteem.

Humility, on the other hand, is not often talked about, and when it is, it seems like they're talking about *humiliation*, not being humble. Being humble means getting taken advantage of, being soft, and getting exploited. Nobody wants that, so we just don't really ever talk about humility.

The pride I'm talking about is having a disdainful view of others; it's vanity and ego and self-centered self-reliance. But the biggest problem with pride is in thinking you can do it without God. Some church people think that humility is thinking poorly of yourself—like you're a wretched sinner with no value or personal worth. However, God's definition of humility is actually pretty different than most of the versions we may hear in church.

Put simply, real humility is being dependent on God, rather than yourself. It's realizing it's *not about you*, it's about *Him*.

Jesus is the ultimate example of humility to us. Paul tells us we are to think of ourselves the way Jesus thought of Himself—He was equal with God, but He didn't think so much of Himself that He had to cling to the advantages that status gave Him. Instead, He came to earth in the humblest way possible and became *human*! As a vulnerable infant born in a cave full of smelly animals, He started a life of serving others, was obedient to His Father, and then died a selfless, horrible death—for us (see Philippians 2:5-8).

Yet this same Jesus is the One who made a whip and drove the money changers and people selling animals out of the Temple. It's the same Jesus who got angry at death and sickness. The same Jesus who directly confronted and condemned the Pharisees for the way they'd misrepresented God to the people. Jesus spoke with power and authority, completely unlike the religious leaders of His day, and His authoritative conviction and charisma drew people by the thousands.

This is no moping, mild, wet noodle Jesus—this is a model of strength under perfect control. Jesus also recognized that even though

He is the Son of God, it wasn't about Him; He gave all credit to God and said only what God told Him to say (see John 12:49).

The word picture for humility is of a powerful horse directed by a small bridle. A two-thousand-pound animal many times the size of its rider is directed and guided by only a small device. It's the same for us—when we're humble and completely God dependent, we can follow His sense of peace and be empowered by His strength.

God Dependent

We have been trained not to depend on anything. We've learned relying on someone else is bad, and when we rely on the things of this world, they do all inevitably disappoint. That is why my favorite definition of humility is actually one that is completely opposite of everything that the world teaches us. **True humility is being God dependent.**

I first started to really learn this when my pastor had me teach some Bible studies, and I had to *really* study the Bible. God used things I learned as core values for my company and as guiding beliefs for my life. Whether in family, business, friendships, or ministry, these things were beliefs about how I was to live and operate. God-dependent humility was one of these core principles.

He began teaching me then that God doesn't just equip us and then send us out to operate independently of Him. God wants us to rely on Him, and as counterintuitive as it sounds, we are at our strongest when we depend solely on His strength, not our own.

In about 2005 my wife and I bought a piece of property in Simi Valley, California, near where we live. However, I soon found out that it was in an earthquake zone—after the fact. For those of you not familiar with the term, an earthquake zone means that it's an area where movements in the earth's crust are common and from which earthquakes may occur. That's the technical definition, but for our purposes, an earthquake zone is an area you can't build on.

When I told Janet about this news, she asked, "Didn't you check to see if it was an earthquake zone before we bought it?" Seems like a no-brainer, right?

"No," I had to admit. "I didn't."

In retrospect, I should have checked, and the people selling it also should have disclosed this information. Understand, I believe in doing your due diligence. However, in hindsight I now see that God had a plan for what was happening—and what He was going to do next.

Janet came to me later and said she'd read that sometimes God healed land. "Do you remember that scripture?" she asked me.

I did: *"If my people, who are called by my name, will humble themselves and pray and seek my face and turn from their wicked ways, then I will hear from heaven, and I will forgive their sin and will heal their land"* (2 Chronicles 7:14).

Janet said, "Let's go on our property. Let's kneel down, raise our hands, and pray that God would heal our land." I didn't see that we had any other options, so we agreed that we would go and lay hands on that property and ask God to heal our land.

So that's exactly what we did—we humbled ourselves, and we prayed and sought God. We believed, and still do, that if we will humble ourselves, it gives God the open door to heal and supernaturally change every area of our lives, which includes where we live.

And we didn't just go out once. We took every praying person we could think of—every minister, pastor, *everyone*—out there to pray with us. We laid out a blanket, kneeled in the mud, and did whatever we had to do. We prayed, and we believed. We also decided that we would never say that we weren't going to be able to build on that land.

Then in 2008 the economy crashed, and we put everything on hold. The land just sat there.

Five years later, we'd already paid off the 12.3 acres we'd bought. We still didn't know if it was a worthless piece of dirt or if we'd ever be able to build on it. As the economy recovered, we decided we needed to find out what kind of land we had—and if God had healed it.

Now, if you want to build in an earthquake zone, you have to dig some trenches—sixty feet long and about thirty feet deep—so they can look at the dirt and tell you if there's a fault there. In a typical twelve-acre area, you might dig three trenches.

We dug nineteen!

There were earthquake faults north of our property. There were earthquake faults south of our property. East, and west, more earthquake zones. And yet when the results of those trenches came back, they were flat out unbelievable—literally, the city didn't believe them! We hired a scientist whose job is to examine these samples, and he said there were *no earthquake faults on our property*! But the city didn't believe it. So, we hired another one, but the city didn't believe him either.

There was *no evidence* of a fault on our land!

For *five years*, we wrestled with the city. Despite all the trenches and all the scientists we hired, who all verified that our land had no evidence of faults, they refused to believe us.

Eventually, I was able to speak to the city planner and city managers, and I told them, "God healed our land!" They laughed a little bit . . . and told us to dig another trench. We dug more trenches for our 12.3 acres than we would've for two hundred acres!

Finally, in November of 2017, we received a document from the city verifying that our land had no earthquake faults.

Above us, earthquake faults. Below us, earthquake faults. But our property *has no earthquake faults*. So, it went from being a worthless piece of dirt to being worth millions of dollars, just like that.

I tell you this story because we had no alternative to God. We were completely dependent on Him, and God completely healed our land as we humbled ourselves and depended solely on Him.

You may remember earlier I said that people in third world countries often have no alternative to God. Think how that drives their prayers, their trust, and, yes, their God-dependent humility. What if—just dream with me here for a moment—we consistently prayed and believed God at His Word, with no backup plans, no excuses, and no reliance on our own ability to make something happen? What if we simply humbled ourselves, got out of the way, and depended on God to come through, no matter what?

I believe we'd see miracles—we'd see God's healing in any and every aspect of our lives. We'd see supernatural businesses changing lives and remaking the workplace. We'd see massive changes in our lives and in the lives of those around us.

And here's the final part to this story. We believe that because of all the prayer that has saturated our property, allowing us to build on it, that the people who eventually live or work there will find their lives unexplainably blessed. We believe they're going to have an encounter with Jesus that will change their lives!

God does not bless us just for us—it's not all about us. He gives to us so we can help others, and it is our prayer that our land will be a great benefit to many people.

The Most Humble Man on Earth

Tradition tells us that Moses wrote the first five books of the Old Testament, and in Numbers 12:3 it says that Moses was the most humble man in the whole world (remember, Moses wrote this about himself). It seems to me that Moses may have invented the humble brag!

If our only definition of humble is that you're lowly and worth-less, then Moses' statement about himself actually disqualifies him.

But if your definition is being God dependent, I can honestly see how Moses may have written this about himself—he was saying that he knew he couldn't do it without God.

Moses told God he couldn't go before Pharaoh and later that he didn't have what it took to lead God's stubborn people. He needed a confidence boost, and he found it by becoming completely dependent on God, because he was putting his trust in God, not himself.

The Bible tells us that God spoke to Moses *"face to face, as one speaks to a friend"* (Exodus 33:11). Moses understood that he couldn't do it without God, and his response was to get very close to Him—so close they spoke "face to face."

Wouldn't you like to be able to say that of your prayer times—that you were so close to God it's like talking face to face with a friend? That's what God wants for us. When you have a relationship like that with God, I think He tells you things He couldn't trust to just anyone. How did Moses write about creation in Genesis? How did he write the books of the Law and give the people so many messages straight from the mouth of God? The Lord had to reveal these things to him, and God could only do that to a humble man dependent on Him.

One of the greatest benefits to humility you can possibly ask for is this kind of face to face, God-dependent relationship. Sadly, many people aren't willing to pursue God like this, and they won't admit that they can't do it without Him. They want to do it on their own—and this is the pride that will keep them from experiencing more of what God wants for their lives.

If you want to have a supernatural business, you must recognize that you cannot do it without God and learn to rely on Him completely.

Duke

Being God dependent looks like being aware of and sensitive to what God is doing. Paul writes to the church in Rome and tells them that God's kids follow His Spirit (check out Romans 8:14). We must operate this way.

I'm a big dog person. In fact, sometimes I like dogs more than people. They love unconditionally, and they're totally reliant on you. Without you, they'd die, and they know it. That's why they come running to greet you when you get home.

In 1997, we were saving to buy our first home. Now, this may sound odd, but because I'm this big dog lover, I wanted to get a dog as a statement of my faith that one day we'd be able to get a house. We'd need a house and a yard for the dog to really enjoy, so getting this dog was like a step of faith for me (that and I wanted a dog!).

So, while we were still in our apartment, I got this puppy, and even when he was little you could tell he was going to be big—he had a huge head and this little body. I brought him home, and Janet said, "What are you doing?"

Understand, at this time all we had was a little cement patio. It's hard to have a big dog when all you have is a cement patio.

But we were believing and trusting God that we'd be able to get a house. And forty-five days after I brought home that dog, we were in escrow for our first house! (Let this be a lesson: If you want a house, go buy a dog.)

We named this dog Duke, and he loved everybody—but he was definitely my dog. He listened to me, and he would mimic every move I made. If I took a step, Duke took a step. If I walked backward, he would follow, and when I stopped, he stopped. Sometimes I'd just mess with him and do a funny little dance.

I didn't specifically train Duke; he was just incredibly attuned to the sound of my voice. If he could hear me, I could call his name from anywhere and he'd immediately come running. He was so well behaved, I liked to take him with me on construction jobs. He'd ride in the back of the truck, and he loved it.

We were starting to get bigger jobs by this point, and I was that contractor with a dog in the back of his truck. Well, one of our new clients was an owner of a big apartment building, and the first day he meets me he tells me, "I really hate those kinds of contractors who have their dog in the back of their pickup."

He told me this *as we walked out toward my truck* . . . where Duke waited. The owner hadn't seen Duke yet, so from seventy-five feet away or more, I softly said and gestured, "Duke, down." Duke had been standing up in the bed, and he laid down immediately. The owner and I walked right past the truck, and he never saw Duke.

Being God dependent is being like Duke—completely attuned to our Master's voice and watching Him for any gesture or direction.

John 15 tells us that God does not call us slaves but instead calls us His friends, yet our only reasonable response to the Creator of the Universe is humble dependence. John then records Jesus' words—without Him, we can do nothing (see John 15:5). But with Him, we can do all things (see Philippians 4:13).

Without Him, we fare no better than a dog if his master does not come home and take care of his every need. We need God for our very next breath.

Humility is acknowledging this fact.

When You Blow It

Sometimes we don't truly understand we are to follow a God direction, Duke-style, until after we've missed it and messed up, and sometimes we just choose to disobey. Recently, a friend asked Janet and me to attend his conference, which was nearby. I made all these excuses because I was really busy. Things at work blew up and it was a really difficult week, but I felt like I was supposed to go.

I was buried beneath a thousand things that needed my attention, not to mention a trip to the East Coast. In my mind, I was telling God all the reasons why I couldn't go. When I talked to Janet about it, she told me it was up to me whether or not we went. I ended up listening to that litany of reasons why I couldn't go instead of the impression God was putting in my heart.

They even texted me the day before the event, telling me they really believed I was supposed to be there! But we didn't go . . .

Immediately after it was over, I *knew* I had messed up. In the next week or so, we experienced all manner of troubles and struggles I am now convinced we could've avoided, had I responded to the prompting to go.

"Conviction" is God letting you know you missed it and communicating to you there's an area of your life where He wants to work on you. We feel unsettled when we don't follow where God is leading us (or make the wrong decision), and it is very different from being punished or feeling God's disapproval. I was convinced that I should have gone to this conference.

So, the question is, when you mess up (and you will), what will you do? Will you humble yourself and acknowledge that you missed it? Or will you make your excuses, get defensive, and push God's correction or guidance away?

None of us are perfect. No one is going to sense the direction of God perfectly 100 percent of the time and always obey and do the right thing. We'd like to think that we will, but we're human. We can learn from these failures. If you will listen to what God is teaching or guiding you to do, you can begin to sense which times were really God leading you and which were just your own thoughts.

Being God dependent means that even when you do not understand, you do it anyway. You may not understand at the moment (or maybe ever), but you learn to obey these nudges from God.

He wants you to *know Him*. He wants you to know Him just as He already knows you, to talk like you were friends face to face (check out 1 Corinthians 13:12).

He cannot do that with a prideful person. But He can do so with someone who is God dependent, ready to move with His slightest word or instruction. As you learn to do that, you will make mistakes. Just make sure you fail forward.

CHAPTER 5:

Don't Be the Opposition

You may remember the supervisor, John, who I nearly fired in the last chapter. I want to tell you more about him. You'll recall that I'd known John most of my life, and he was an outstanding employee. So it broke my heart when he told me that he and his wife were getting a divorce.

"That's a tragedy!" I told him. "I'd love to see you guys work it out."

"No, it's over," he told me.

I felt something confident rise up inside me, and I said, "You know what? I believe that you guys are going to get back together."

He replied, "That's nice, and I'd love to, but it just doesn't look like it's going to happen."

Every time I saw John, I'd tell him that I thought he and his wife were going to get back together. This went on for *years*! He'd say, "Mike, I'm with someone else now," or, "We're divorced!" But something in me just wouldn't let it go.

For about four years, I spoke life into his marriage more times than I can count. Finally, one day John called me on a Saturday and asked if he could come to my office. Saturday is my private day where I spend two or three hours in the office alone, often praying over the company. I don't like to be bothered, so at first I resisted. "What do you need?" I asked him bluntly.

"Can I just please come talk to you?" he asked.

So he came by, and he sat right across from me. "Will you pray with me?" he asked. "I want to accept Jesus and become a Christian."

I almost fell out of my chair! John was a good friend, but he was as rough as they come. He was a hard-core construction guy, with a filthy mouth and lots of nasty habits. He'd been my friend for many years, and I wondered if he'd ever come around.

And now he was sitting in my office asking for help!

I happily prayed with him, and he lifted up his hands and accepted Jesus into his life. Then when he was done he said, "Oh, yeah, my wife and I got back together again."

This hardened man, a rough-talking, bad-behaving construction worker, came to me to ask for help accepting Jesus. He knew that he needed God. That took some serious humility.

John came to Jesus about a year *after* the story I told you in the previous chapter where I almost fired him. Humility opened the door for us to experience that moment together. But I think it was humility that also helped him put his marriage back together and start following Jesus. We do not heal old wounds by being prideful; only humility can bring healing like this.

When I think of the example of John coming to Jesus and seeing his marriage restored, I have to wonder how many things God does not have the opportunity to do in our lives because we close the door with our pride.

Pride has consequences. They are natural, not punishments; our selfish arrogance keeps us from experiencing God's best. The worst part is, He told us all about the consequences of pride in the Bible. But are we listening?

God Said It in Triplicate

I'm going to teach you something about reading the Bible. It's really complicated: **When God says something, listen to Him. Then do it.**

Now, if it's in the Bible *twice*, pay twice as much attention! If it's in there *three times*, it's like God IS SHOUTING IN ALL CAPS!

In James 4:6, James quotes, *"God opposes the proud but shows favor to the humble"* from Proverbs 3:34. A few verses later, James writes that we are to humble ourselves before the Lord, and He will lift us up.

Then, just in case you missed it, Peter quotes the *very same* Proverbs 3:34 again in 1 Peter 5:5![1]

When we're proud, it's like we've gone to the other team and now we're on the opposite side of Him. We've left Him. I don't know about you, but I want to be on *God's* team. He is my MVP, and I know that I will not see long-term success in life or in business without Him.

If God talked about humility and pride so many times in the Bible, we must listen! God is urgently trying to get a point across to you, and it's so important that He has filled His Word with the encouragement to be humble and dependent on Him, not leaning on your own understanding (see Proverbs 3:5).

So how do we actually live more humbly and depend on God instead of ourselves? He showed me a few ways, and I'd like to share them with you.

Own Your Mistakes

In my industry, I work for a lot of people who are less concerned about getting a project completed than they are about how they look

---

[1]   See also Job 22:29, Psalm 138:6, Proverbs 29:23, and Matthew 23:12 if you want some other examples.

to their boss or their boss's boss. When situations come up (and they always do because construction is not an exact science), some of these construction managers will spend thousands upon thousands of dollars covering up and misleading so it doesn't appear that a situation is their fault. The irony is, oftentimes we could just *fix* the mistake for hundreds of dollars, not thousands.

At MRC, we have built a brand out of simply fixing problems. Instead of wasting time pointing fingers and assessing blame, or being concerned with how we're perceived, we just fix things. If it's our fault, we quickly own it, come up with a solution, and move past it.

It requires humility to own up to what's happened and then get busy making it right. Too often, we want to protect ourselves, and we think pride is the answer. It is not.

A former assistant of mine was supposed to book me at a hotel in Florida, where I do a lot of work. I was busy until late that night, and I got to my favorite hotel close to 10:00 p.m. to find out they didn't have a room reserved for me.

I called my assistant, trying to fix the problem, and apparently when she canceled another reservation, somehow mine got canceled too. I told her I didn't care whose fault it was and to just get me a room. "I will fix this," she told me.

But I later learned that she then spent the next three hours trying to convince the hotel staff that the mistake wasn't her fault. After all those hours, they couldn't get me a room, and at 1:30 in the morning I ended up having to drive for about half an hour to take the last room we could find nearby, a smoking room, where I managed to eke out a couple of hours of sleep.

The thing is, there were plenty of rooms nearby hours before, when we first found out about the problem. If she'd been less concerned about the appearance of fault, and more interested in getting the problem solved, I could've been in a room getting some sleep.

Pride kept her from handling the issue. Sometimes it can cost you your job.

Pride will make you more worried about how you look than what you're doing. It will prevent you from fixing the real issue while you try to do damage control on your image. Humbling yourself and owning up to mistakes—or even taking responsibility for those that aren't actually yours—and then working for a solution will give you a better reputation than any image management your pride can do.

God taught me this firsthand. Some of the owners I work with are very wealthy and extremely arrogant, and they can be very demanding.

I was working for one of those owners on a particular occasion, and we did part of his building as a mock-up of what the rest of his buildings would look like. Our work looked spectacular, but this owner got upset about the pricing of one of the components of the job. Apparently, he just went off—yelling and screaming and ranting. He called me on the phone and yelled, "You guys are fired!" He wasn't going to pay for the $50,000 worth of work we'd already done. Not only that, he said he was going to sue me to put his building back the way it was.

First, I figured out what had happened—he was apparently upset about the pricing of some scaffolding. I eventually was satisfied that this problem wasn't my employee's fault; this guy was just being completely unreasonable.

The whole situation would put us in a really bad place as a company, so we began seeking God in prayer. I told my prayer team what was happening, because I knew that when we get people praying together, the supernatural happens.

My pastor suggested that I try fasting (which I don't like because it means skipping eating and replacing with praying), and I was so desperate I decided to try it. As we prayed and fasted, I felt like God wanted me to humble myself.

I didn't know what He meant, but I felt like I was to call the owner. So I got him on the phone, and he grudgingly agreed to meet with me face to face. As I drove over, I was praying for God to show me what to do.

I walked in to find him and about five of his executives waiting. He was still mad—yelling and cussing—then we sat down, and I told him, "I'm here to say I'm sorry for whatever miscommunication we had and whatever part my company played to get us to this. I'd like to do the job, but I'd like to first just tell you I'm sorry."

There was complete silence in the room, and then he yelled, "*Everybody out!*" So I got up and started walking out, but he barked, "Not you. You stay."

When everyone else was out of the room, he said, "I never wanted to fire you. I got upset, but I do not show weakness. I want you to do the job, and I appreciate you coming in here. It helped me to save face." That day he signed the contract with MRC—a three-million-dollar job. It ended up being one of the most successful jobs that we ever did.

It never would've happened if I had not humbled myself.

Listen to Your Spouse

You'll remember that earlier in the book I told you that there are some people you must decide in advance to listen to. When they speak into your life, you've already determined you'll listen to them.

Well, one place I struggle when it comes to humility—and I think many of us struggle like this—is humbly listening to things my wife points out. Sometimes these are issues where I have a blind spot. Sometimes I just did something without thinking. But for whatever reason, it can be very hard to take constructive criticism from our spouses.

I've struggled with this over the years, but as I have matured and God has helped me with humility, I have started thinking, "Do I need to be right all the time? Or do I want to hear from God?" Because I will tell you this: God will speak to you through the voice of your spouse, and you ignore it at your own risk.

It's very humbling to receive constructive feedback from your spouse when you've messed up. It hurts your pride, but it has a tremendous amount of value and importance. Learning to receive feedback puts you in a position to be in a supernatural business.

Just Let It Go

Sometimes when it's not our fault, we get hurt, and pride can rise up like a defense mechanism. I remember that one time in the late 90s, I did some projects with a guy I was friends with at church. The problem was, he wasn't good with his money, and I wasn't good at noticing he wasn't good with his money. So, while he got paid 90 percent for these jobs up front, he ran out of money when he was only about half complete. We got into an argument, and he ended up walking off the job!

Our pastor intervened, and he called me on my anger toward this guy. He told me, "Mike, you're clearly not in the wrong, but if you'll forgive him, God will take care of you."

I didn't want to forgive him. I was angry! *Furious!* I had to watch as he sat up at the front in the church, raising his hands praising God . . . while I wondered if I could hit him with my Bible if I threw it at his head!

I just couldn't let it go. He'd ripped me off, and I had no way of finishing the jobs. I felt like I was carrying a weight around my shoulders, bearing me down.

I ended up talking to my pastor again, and he asked, "Have you asked Jesus to help you?"

I thought, "What good is that going to do?" But I did it—not to be religious but because I had no other ideas. I prayed and asked Jesus to help me. I asked Him to help me forgive.

Forgiveness is both a decision and a process. I made the decision then: I would forgive this guy. But then the process began, and God started working on my feelings.

In the meantime I had to finish the project. I put out an ad for help, and one day I got this little card. It said, "My name is Manuel. I need a job. If you don't like my work, you don't have to pay me."

So we scheduled a time to meet at the first job I needed to finish, and I was running a little late because I had to go pick up supplies. I pulled up to find that this guy, Manuel, had gotten started . . . and was already halfway done, using his own materials! Over the next five or six weeks, Manuel and I finished all the jobs, just the two of us working together.

We became friends, and I saw that he was very good at what he did. He also knew some guys who needed jobs, and they were good at what they did, too! First his brother, then his cousin, and then more. Eventually, Manuel ran a crew of twenty-five guys for me. They were *amazing*!

They *loved me*. I asked why one time, and Manuel said with a smile, "You pay us!" It turns out, they'd been ripped off, just like I had. One time they told me it was their goal to make me rich!

Once, when I brought them all lunch, as I drove away I prayed, "God, thank You for these guys." I felt as though the Lord answered, "When you forgave, I sent you Manuel."

There is an incredible, supernatural grace and power in forgiveness. It will transform your life and business, and when you humble yourself and forgive, you open the door for God to bless you.

Manuel still works with me. We've all prospered. Best of all, Manuel accepted Jesus, and he became a powerful evangelist and has led over 250 people to Jesus in the last twenty years. Your humility, and forgiveness, will produce fruit years down the line.

Under Authority

Becoming God dependent is especially important—and often difficult—when God has given you some success in business. When we're in positions of authority and responsibility, it's easy to think that we got there on the back of our own hard work and smarts, when in fact we can do nothing without Him.

Success in business brings influence, and if we're not careful, that can go to our heads. People may treat us with respect, listen more attentively when we talk, and value our advice more. If you don't recognize that God has given you the ability to make wealth, that you can only do all things thanks to Him, and that you're just as dependent on God for your next breath as everyone else, you can get a swollen head.

You'd better watch out, because we just learned God *opposes* the proud! So how do we prevent this? One technique is to make sure you are under godly authority.

Janet and I felt that we were to submit to our first pastor, because we believe that it's important to be under his spiritual covering and authority. I gave the church my schedule for the month, so they'd know when I was in town and when I was traveling, and we felt like this was an important part of being submitted to authority. Our pastor has held me accountable, and when we later moved to a different church, I did the same thing with our new pastor.

I asked him to call me on anything he ever saw in my life that was less than God's standard of integrity and humility. It surprised him. Many other successful people want concessions and special treatment. If we instead pursue humility and accountability, it can help insulate us from pride.

Humility eventually brings authority, because we can only have authority when we are under authority (see Matthew 8:9-11). You may be the boss at work, but you can help protect your life and cultivate humility by intentionally submitting yourself to spiritual authority. There's protection in humility.

If you're not successful yet, don't think that lets you off the hook. Some of the most prideful people I've ever met were those *trying to move up*. They wanted to be seen as big shots, so they act like they think big shots should act—but they haven't really even accomplished anything yet!

We can tend to act prideful, when deep inside, we are secretly insecure. We tend to be insecure when we are reliant on ourselves instead of God. God has shown me that making sure we give Him credit helps us to stay humble.

As I started to move forward and make strides toward operating a supernatural business, I craved recognition. I wanted to be recognized for what I was doing, and I probably even tried to look more successful than I was at times.

It's not bad to get recognition, but striving for recognition because you need it to feel good about yourself is definitely pride. The truth of the matter is that the more successful you get, the less you actually want recognition. It can end up being pretty frustrating, and in many cases you just want to be under the radar. Instead of craving people's awareness of what you're doing, the solution is to point them to the One who really deserves all the credit.

Point to God

I remember a conversation I had one time with my uncles. It was the year 2000, and they were at our house. They said, "Mike, you and Janet are doing really well. We're really proud of you."

I responded, "Well, we've worked really hard, and we've tried to make the right decisions." Right then, I felt like God was like, "What about Me?"

I didn't really mean to be prideful, but we would never have been in that position of expanding success had God not started teaching us about things like integrity, giving us His favor, and supernatural business. Part of being humble is not taking credit ourselves and instead pointing back to God.

I've heard countless people receive a compliment and then disingenuously say, "Well, you know, it's all God." I don't mean we're supposed to be disingenuous like that. It may take practice, but it's worth it: Take off the mask, be humble and transparent, and tell people that you could never have gotten to where you are without God.

If nothing else, consider this—none of us is an island. We'd never become successful without the help of people around us. I know I never would have gotten where I am today without Janet, my senior vice president, Dave, and many others.

I've had people tell me that Dave is the best guy in construction that they have ever met. If I were insecure about it and full of pride, that could make me feel resentful. One time early on, I remember someone telling me, "Without him, your company would be nothing." I walked out of the room going, "God, what about me?"

I felt like God told me this: "That *is* you." When people around you do well, it's the same as *you* doing well. The more you recognize that the success of *others* is actually *your* success, the better you will do in business—and the more likely you'll be to stay humble.

Be very hesitant to take credit and very quick to point out the awesomeness in other people and the goodness of God, because both of those things are like anti-pride treatments for your soul. Every time someone gives you a compliment, practice reminding yourself that you are God dependent. Don't be fake; really pause and remind yourself that it's not all about you. Remember that you're reliant on God for even your next breath and that you can do nothing without Him.

Do You Have a Problem?

One of the most insidious things about pride is that when we're full of it, we're very unlikely to confess it to someone. We think we've got it all together, and we can even try to convince ourselves that we're *not* prideful—but that's because we're too proud to ask for help! Yet the only way we're going to get over it is to admit we need help from God and others who love us.

It reminds me of my stepfather. In 1990, my mom was the first one in our family to get clean and sober. I was still on drugs when she got clean and started a twelve-step program. In 1992, I became a Christian and had an encounter with God and was delivered from drug addiction, but I wasn't involved in a twelve-step and was into church instead. My mom came to know Jesus about two years later. Over time, all the members of my family became born-again Christians—everyone except my stepdad. Everyone got off drugs, except my stepdad (though he eventually did get saved in 2010).

My mom is an incredible woman and was very patient, but finally she told him, "You've got to get sober!" The drugs had altered his mind, but he refused to admit he had a problem. He'd tell us that *we* were the ones with problems and that he never had a problem with drugs or alcohol, so it was fine for us to need to get sober and to meet Jesus, but he didn't need it.

Eventually, my mom had to leave. He wouldn't get help; he didn't think he needed it. It cost him his marriage to an amazing, godly woman.

Don't let your pride cost you.

In the Bible, God says repeatedly—if you're full of pride, He will oppose you. I don't know about you, but I don't want God opposing me! I want to be on His team.

Pride is a condition. It's like being sick. When you're sick, you get treatment, and you get better. Pride is no different. You don't want to be infected with it; it'll sabotage every good thing in your life, as it did for my stepfather.

If you're struggling in this area, start by admitting it to God. The Bible tells us that we are to confess our sins to one another so that we can be healed (James 5:16). You need people in your life who can call you on it if they see it.

You can start right now—tell God about it. Confess to Him, "God, I have a problem with pride, and I need Your help. Please teach me how to live in humility." Talk to your pastor or a trusted friend, own mistakes, forgive, and submit yourself to the authority of trusted individuals you empower to hold you accountable.

It's worth it. Humility is the path to being lifted up by God, and the heights He wants for you are so much greater than where you can get bootstrapping yourself up with pride. If you want God to lift you up, it's time to leave the weight of pride behind and instead experience power under perfect control.

CHAPTER 6:

Helping Others Is the Key to Greatness

A supernatural business requires that we serve one another—our clients, employees, and others—with a spirit that only comes when we have spent time with Jesus in prayer. You cannot truly serve God's way if you're not humble and dependent on Him and practicing integrity. If you try to do it on your own, you'll quickly exhaust your resources of energy, patience, and grace. We need God empowering us to serve the way He's called us to help.

God showed me this at different times in my life, and one time in particular God showed me how humility and service intersect. We'd been working with a great client, a multi-billion-dollar company, for a few years when they hired a brilliant new project manager. He told me, "Mike, I'm going to start doing these renovations at a higher level than our company has ever done before."

"Great," I answered. "I want to be part of it."

He said, "On this project we don't have the budget for what I want to do. Can you help me get there?" I told him we absolutely could, so we began to work together to come up with ways of being more cost-effective to free up money for other things he wanted to do. We made significant progress in getting him where he wanted, but he had a few other things that there was just not enough in the budget to do.

"Can you help me get any further?" he asked.

I had to answer, "I can't do this all for free. I've already given you everything I can, and I can't give you more than that."

"Tell you what," he replied. "We have a new project coming up, and if you help me out on this project, you'll be able to make it up on the next project. The next project has a much bigger budget, but first I have to finish this one."

I was skeptical—and I was right to be. I quickly learned that every project has to pay for itself and that if something isn't in writing, it doesn't exist. But at that point, I was still growing in business, so I agreed to do what he wanted, as this kind of practice isn't uncommon in construction.

A couple of weeks later, this new manager asked if I'd come by the corporate office. I thought I was going to sign the new contract, but instead he told me that while they were delighted with the project we'd just finished, they were awarding the new job to another contractor.

I completely lost my temper. I was absolutely furious, and it wasn't a pretty scene. When I got downstairs, I felt like God gave me a verse: "*Whatever happens, conduct yourselves in a manner worthy of the gospel of Christ . . .* " (Philippians 1:27a).

Whatever happens . . .

God wanted me to conduct myself like the new person I was (not the guy who sold drugs at the back gate of the high school), no matter what happened. I immediately felt convicted about my anger, and I called my office to dictate an email to my assistant (this was before smartphones). "Heather, I just lost my temper with a multi-billion-dollar company. They ripped me off. I want to send an email to them, and I want it to say, 'I'm sorry that I was so furious at you, but you ripped me off.' But it has to sound professional."

She suggested, "Let's try this: 'I apologize for my outburst, but I do believe my concerns were justified.'" That sounded good, so I had her send that.

While God was still busy dealing with me on this issue and my anger, she told me, "He just emailed you back." I had her read it to me. It said, "I'm not sure why you are so upset. Maybe we could talk about this more shortly."

I was suddenly mad all over again! But I kept leaning into God, not out of religious obligation but because being angry is not a productive way to live and doesn't feel good. I felt like the Lord told me, "Let it go."

He was teaching me to be humble and what it takes to serve—letting go of offense. He was also showing me a principle for every supernatural business: You have to be willing to let it go. When you're upset, you cannot operate in the supernatural; you can't even work too well in the natural! Stuff is going to happen, and we must learn to let it go and trust God when things aren't going the way we want. Let our target be behaving like Jesus: "*When they hurled their insults at him, he did not retaliate; when he suffered, he made no threats. Instead, he entrusted himself to him who judges justly*" (1 Peter 2:23).

Be Gracious

About a week later, this new construction manager called me. "Mike, the other contractor can't do about 10 percent of the job. It's out of his area of expertise. Would you be willing to do 10 percent of the job?"

It was like a slap in the face. I felt like God urged me to be gracious. So, I answered, through a grimace he couldn't see over the phone, "I'd love to do that 10 percent of the job."

Another week later, he called me again. By now, I'd moved past my anger over the situation, legitimately having let it go. He told me, "Mike, I just found out that there's another 5 percent of the job the contractor can't do."

I answered, "I'm already doing the 10 percent; of course, I'll do the other 5." At this point, I'd moved on, so this time it was easy to be gracious to him.

As if on cue, a week after that he called me again! He asked if I was still in the office (it was 6:30 p.m.), and I was, so we agreed that he would come by to talk. He plopped himself down in a chair in my office and admitted, "It turns out the contractor can't do 100 percent of the job. He's just not qualified. Are you willing to do the full job?"

I said, "Absolutely."

He said, "I know that you made concessions on the other job, so we'll give you the contract plus an additional fifty grand." Later we signed the contract, and it ended up being a tremendously successful job. Through all of this, God taught me so much.

However, that isn't the best part. Six months later, that new manager called me and said, "Hey, Mike, I just want to let you know last week I went to church and raised my hand to accept Jesus. You were the first person I wanted to call and tell. The way you treated me on that project played a huge part in my decision to become a Christian."

As a brilliant architect, he has since helped build multiple churches and has become a very dear friend. He and his wife are on the board at their church, and he's been a part of many ministry events I've done over the years. That relationship would never have flourished if God hadn't helped me deal with my anger. Because I humbled myself, we were able to serve this company and this manager in a way that built a long-lasting friendship and connection between our companies.

Helping others is the key to greatness. Jesus put it clearly: If anyone wants to be great, if anyone wants to be first, if anyone wants to be a leader, you must take the position of a servant (see Matthew 20:25-27). Jesus even says that He "*did not come to be served, but to serve . . .* " (Matthew 20:28). If that was Jesus' view of Himself, and we are to be like Him, then we can confidently say that it is our calling to serve others the same way He did.

Change the Atmosphere

From time to time, I've felt like I was just organizing construction projects, and I knew that wasn't my true calling. I remember asking God, "What is my job?" I feel like God told me my job is to position the people that I work with to succeed. My job is to serve the people I work with. You may recall God telling me that when people around you do well, it's the same as you doing well—this is what He meant.

When we began to study what our vendors and subcontractors needed, we realized they just wanted to get paid when we said we'd pay them! I can still remember being a subcontractor and not being able to get general contractors to pay me—and even following people home just trying to get paid. So I decided that when I became the general contractor, I would get my people paid. When they've been paid and aren't worried about money, people work better. Happy people have more creative ideas about how to get projects done effectively and efficiently.

Proverbs tells us not to withhold good when it's in our power to act (Proverbs 3:27), and now at MRC we can get our people paid even faster than we get paid ourselves. As I write this, in my area there is more work for subcontractors than they can do, so they get to pick and choose where they work. They decide to work with us because of how we treat them, but I didn't start treating them right during this current economy. I started many years ago, and we are currently enjoying the benefits of having served our subcontractors and vendors by simply getting them paid quickly.

We learned our subcontractors and vendors also needed production to make a profit. I spend time praying for my subcontractors and my vendors, and God started showing me that my job was to add value to them. So, we instruct our superintendents that while most bosses lord their position over their people, we want ours to serve those who work for us. There's a short-term increase to pummeling a subcontractor into submission on a project, but there is a long-term gain to be had by creating a working environment with a good atmosphere.

The best atmosphere is a collaborative relationship between the owner, us, the subcontractors, and the vendors. That collaborative atmosphere is only found where there's a win-win attitude.

If I'm trying to make the owners win, if I'm trying to make the subs win, and if I'm trying to add value to my employees, that creates an atmosphere on our projects where the supernatural happens. In fact, I am on a mission to change the atmosphere in my home, at my church, in my relationships, at work, at my job sites, and everywhere else I go. I want them to have a positive atmosphere.

Look for Ways to Serve

If the atmosphere around you isn't supernatural, try being a servant in those areas. What can you do? I like to find out what someone is trying to accomplish and to learn their number one goal. What's their endgame? I have learned that every job is different, and priorities can change even when working with the same owners.

It seems like it should not need to be said, but my first responsibility in serving my clients is to execute the contract we've signed to the letter. It amazes me how many people don't understand that when you agree to work for someone, you work *for* them! But it goes deeper: My calling with my clients is to learn what they need and want to accomplish and then help them do it. I want to get behind their vision and help them execute it—that is serving them.

One of the greatest ways we have the opportunity to serve MRC is that I sit back at my desk as the president of the company and I think this way: "What do I want for myself?" And "What can I do to make that available for the people that work for MRC?"

When I was a younger businessperson and I had young kids and wanted to go to their games, I needed to take time off to go to their games or to a parent/teacher conference. So we initiated flex time, giving people the opportunity to be at the office any time between 7:00 a.m. and 5:00 p.m. (while still working eight hours a day and not having to use PTO). If they needed to take a two-hour lunch or they needed to come in later one day they could. Real life happens, and people need the opportunity to do the things they need to do to manage their lives. I found that when people were able to do that, it was a weight off their shoulders. Actually, people work better when they don't have to worry about things. I also like to take time off and be with my family, so we gave MRC employees benefits like giving them an extra paid day off at Christmastime so they could spend more time with their families.

We've always tried to bring people to another level. We do that by mentoring and coaching. It started naturally from me to the people who were directly underneath me. We made it our company culture, as supervisors, to find people that we're supervising who want to go to another level and then spend time with them by teaching and leading them. We've had many laborers at MRC become foremen and then superintendents, and we've had this culture of growth from inside. I think that has been one of the greatest ways we serve people, by giving them an opportunity to grow in their career. Everyone wants to grow in their careers.

We've tried to create a different atmosphere on the job sites, so we've had vendors that give us different products. We've raffled them off and given them away on the jobs, and it gives some excitement on the jobs. We've looked for ways to give bonuses for employees who are doing well, buying them tools and other gear. When they have more tools, it puts them in a position where they can grow in their career and increase their wages.

We're consistently trying to do things that we believe will add value to people. Our guys drive long distances to work, so we set up a carpool policy. When you drive with another person to work, the company will reimburse 50 percent of your gas. We did this when gas had gone up to over $5 a gallon. When we did this, over 50 percent of our employees started carpooling.

There was a cap to the 50 percent reimbursement for two in the car, so we added that we'd do 100 percent reimbursement for having a third person in the car. This was such a good deal for our workers that within three months, 80 percent of our people were carpooling.

That obviously saved them a tremendous amount of money and added a great deal of value to them. In the overall scheme, it did not end up costing MRC a terrible amount of money. By doing this, we added a lot of value to the workers. Even until this day, the carpool and reimbursement are still going on.

Later, my pastor shared that a family at our church had a son at UCLA who did a case study on MRC's gas reimbursements. UCLA thought it was such a great idea and made so much sense for business, they ended up using it as a case study.

Around 2002 or 2003, one of my long-term employees met with me and said he was having some difficulties in his marriage. He thought that he and his wife might break up. I asked him what the problem was. He said his wife thought that he was cheating on her. So, I asked the obvious question: "Are you cheating on your wife?" He said that he wasn't cheating on his wife but that his mother-in-law was telling his wife that he was cheating on her. His father-in-law had cheated on his mother-in-law, so she was constantly telling his wife that he was unfaithful and to keep a close eye on him.

I had an opportunity, a job that was two hundred miles away in Northern California. So, I offered to move him and his family up there so that would give them some distance away from the in-laws. I hoped maybe that would help with his family. He went home and talked it over with his wife and decided they wanted to try it. They ended up falling back deeply in love with each other! They had two sons and ended up having a daughter. This distance between them and his in-laws positively impacted their marriage. It added value to their family, and all I did was offer an opportunity to him. As a company, if we think that way and act intentionally to serve our employees, it creates a culture that attracts the right people.

Serving Clients

I have learned that serving clients looks different from one job to the next. Sometimes serving a client means helping them accomplish something as quickly as possible—even if that costs more money. I've had people ask if we can get a job done quicker, even though we have a schedule that matches a contract. But one time I had a client that offered us an extra $150,000 if we could get a project done sixty days early. We changed the schedule, so they could put that job together with other work they were financing—a service that really helped them and me.

A contract is what you're obliged to do, but serving means finding ways to go above and beyond. Don't you love it when people do that for you? When my assistant goes beyond the mundane details of her role and looks to fulfill what I need to be done to help me, I take notice. That takes intentionality and a service mind-set, and it changes the equation.

At MRC, we're always looking for ways to serve our clients. That may mean finding out that a client needs to rent out their three-bedroom units and moving those to the highest priority to get them done first to meet that need. Because of our experience, we can see areas where our clients may be exposed, and we try to help educate them and develop ways to solve those problems.

The first job I did for that multi-billion-dollar company, I was just getting my feet wet doing multi-family buildings. I was very excited because this was my first really big project, and I was learning about this concept of service. But when I told them that I was excited to be on the job and wanted to help them succeed, they responded cynically because everyone *says* they want to help, but their experience was that contractors only wanted their money.

However, I convinced them I genuinely wanted to help them succeed, and they admitted that they were exposed. Senior management didn't think they could do the project and weren't sure they'd get the returns they wanted. The two mid-level managers we were working with feared they could be fired if the project wasn't done in six months. They told me, "We're rooting for you. We don't trust you, but we're rooting for you."

When I talked to my crew leader, we did the math and found that it was going to take thirty-eight weeks, which was twelve weeks too long. Worse, because we had to allow for drying time and inspections, it just flat out took a week per building, and there was no way to get a building done faster, unless we had more than one crew working.

We'd need a second crew doing a separate building if we were to get it done in time. Since early in my career, I have designed my company around our clients' needs, so we did what we had to do—we hired another crew. (In fact, MRC earned a reputation for getting things done faster than anyone else partly because of things like this.)

In the end, we didn't deliver the buildings to them in twenty-six weeks as they needed. We actually did it in only *nineteen* weeks!

The multi-billion-dollar company gave us every job they had for the next seven years, and one of those mid-level managers got promoted to senior manager to junior vice president to senior vice president.

Best of all, when I invited him to our church, he agreed, and he ended up raising his hand and accepting Jesus! The other mid-level manager went a different route and started his own company, and when he needed a junior partner to do some construction work he ended up asking me to join him. I learned many things from him that are of great value to me today, and I'm still friends with both of these men.

When you're in a contract, you're obligated to do what you've agreed to or what you're told, but being a servant means going beyond and actively looking for ways to add value to the relationship. It means going beyond the minimum and actively finding ways to serve their true needs better.

Pride Prevents Service

We covered integrity and humility first because you cannot serve effectively without working on those two. I know this firsthand. The excellent relationship we had with that multi-billion-dollar company came to an end because I didn't model these things in service to them and learned a costly lesson.

The construction manager at that time wanted us to do some swift work on some apartment buildings so that they could sell them within a particular time frame—basically as quickly as possible. We didn't need permits or anything to do the work we were doing, and we also were not going to fix some of the imperfections we would ordinarily correct as we worked, but that was because the construction manager wanted it that way, so that we could do it quicker. We did one building, and he liked the work and told us to do the same thing to the other structures involved in the project.

Well, he got promoted, and the man who replaced him went out on a job site and noticed that this wasn't the same quality of work they were accustomed to from MRC. I tried to tell him that we weren't repairing some things because his boss wanted us to do it faster, but he hadn't gotten that memo. All he knew was that it wasn't up to our usual standards.

The construction manager who'd been promoted was now too busy to come down to the job site, so he sent a representative. Again, I told him what we'd worked out with his boss, but he didn't know about it either. The superintendent for the project told me flat out, "Listen, I'm not accepting it."

I lost my temper with him. "You just need to shut up. You don't know what happened." Well, first of all, it's never a good idea to tell the person you work for to "shut up." It's bad business. I was being prideful; I was not looking for a way to serve them, I was just frustrated.

Even though I was "right," and we were doing what we'd been told, I was wrong to treat him like that instead of serving him, and it cost me. That superintendent blackballed us with the multi-billion-dollar company that helped establish our business, and it ended a very fruitful seven-year relationship. I haven't worked for them since.

Obviously, this was not serving God's way. This was indulging my own pride, and it cost me. Pride prevents true service. We're supposed to serve people because they each have incredible value to God, not because they "deserve it."

Ultimately, we are to serve others as though we were serving God. Paul writes, "*Serve wholeheartedly, as if you were serving the Lord, not people, because you know that the Lord will reward each one for whatever good they do . . .*" (Ephesians 6:7-8).

To Serve and Protect

Earlier, I mentioned that part of serving our clients is that we help them when they're exposed, such as the two managers at that multi-billion-dollar company whose jobs likely depended on our project going well. In serving them well, we protected them, and this is one way that MRC has made a reputation.

But it isn't just for our clients. My senior vice president, Dave, makes it his job to protect me and our company—which in turn protects all our employees, vendors, and subcontractors by keeping us in business. As I've mentioned, he holds me accountable, and Dave is well known for being one of the best and brightest individuals anyone knows in construction.

I remember one time when Dave and I went to San Diego, which is far from our office, to check out a project we were working on for a new client. We immediately noticed that there were problems, and Dave said, "Mike, one of us needs to stay here. I'm better at this kind of stuff, so why don't you leave me here?"

I got on a train to head back home . . . and Dave headed to Walmart to buy some clean underwear. We hadn't packed anything, since we hadn't expected to stay down there. Dave was serving the company, but he was also serving me because he knows he's better at that type of work. (It's the same way if I ever go boating—Dave knows I'm not technical, so he makes sure he goes with me because he doesn't want me to hurt myself!)

Serving and protecting is some of the best job security you could ever have. Dave is actually the one who helped me start in multi-family dwelling work by bringing me in when he was at this large company back in the mid 90s. So, when he became available, we teamed up in September of 2000 and haven't looked back. We have been serving clients, one another, and the company ever since, and God has used that to allow MRC to touch many lives.

Serve Through Prayer

Prayer is the most significant way to add value, to help, and to minister to those around you. I saved this for last because prayer is not to be a substitute for physically serving people. It is, however, the ultimate way in which we serve, because as I mentioned before, prayer is the cornerstone of a supernatural business.

In 2004, my pastor called me and told me that the Lord had shown him that if I would spend a significant time in prayer, then God would show me something about what I was to do in the next season of my life. I've always believed in honoring what my pastor tells me, as he is a person of influence in my life, so I began praying during my drive to and from work. It took me about fifteen to twenty minutes each way, so I started praying during those times in addition to my regular times.

After I had been doing this for about a month, God began to show me something—that just as I was to be the spiritual leader at home, I was to be the spiritual leader at my business as well. This is a crucial component to having a supernatural business.

Everyone wants someone else looking out for them. I began to learn that I was that person for my employees—I wanted what's best for them, what would be good for them, and things that would help them. I found out that one of the most significant ways I could serve the people I work with—employees, customers, vendors, and subcontractors—was by praying for them. I prayed they would make the right decisions and that they would have good things happen in their lives.

With my clients, I at first was praying that they would send me more jobs, but I felt like the Lord asked me, "Do you think that's what's important to Me?" It changed the way I prayed, and I began to pray that they would come to know Him. If they did know God, I asked that they get to know Him better. I prayed for their families, for their marriages, and for their kids—anything I could think of.

Praying for people changes the ways in which you serve them, and you will love those you pray for. Love changes the way we treat people and how we interact with them, and people can feel its authenticity.

When you genuinely love people, they can tell. I know this because while I was in the Dominican Republic meeting with the churches Janet and I helped start, I started talking with one of the guys, David, from the churches who is on our prayer team. Really, David's job is to pray for Janet and me, our businesses, and our kids. I was driving with David, and he said, "Mike, I really love you."

I said, "Oh, that's very nice."

Then he said it again: "Mike, I just really, really love you."

I said, "Oh, that's really, super nice." Then he said it a third time, and I was feeling a little bit weird because he's a guy and I'm a guy, and he kept telling me how much he loved me. After he said that, he goes, "It's not possible to pray for someone as much as I pray for you and not love you."

You will love those you pray for. So, who are you praying for?

For my vendors, I began praying that their jobs would be successful and asking that they'd have creative ideas. I prayed that they would enjoy increased profits and good cash flow, and I asked God that they would have ideas on how to do their jobs better and faster.

The more I prayed for others, the more God began to do these things for me as well. At first, I didn't realize what was happening, but one day I was in my office praying for my vendors when I realized that I had three jobs where we'd experienced increased profits—the very thing I was asking God to do for them.

I did not begin praying for others so that I would experience God's goodness, but I will be honest: When I realized the connection, it made me even more passionate about how I prayed for them! We do not serve so that we may be blessed, but serving others, especially by praying for them, has a natural outcome from God—good things happening for us and for them.

Not only did we watch others being blessed as we prayed, but we have seen over one thousand people and counting come to know

Jesus through our company. People have been healed, and we've seen marriages put back together. God has set people free, blessed them outrageously, and transformed their lives—and we have had a role in it all by praying for them.

I told you a supernatural business starts with prayer, but it isn't just prayer for your business. You may begin there, but do not stop there. Serve everyone your business touches through prayer. As you authentically serve them and pray, you will watch God do amazing things in their lives—and in yours.

CHAPTER 7:

Take Courage

Real courage isn't the absence of fear. Courage is when you experience the fear . . . and do it anyway. Fear wants you to believe what it says instead of what God says is true. It takes both faith and courage in God to press through and overcome it.

One of the biggest fears humans have is that of the unknown. We fear what we do not understand, and I can remember when God began working on this fear within me. It was about 2000, and MRC had just experienced the breakthrough of the big job with that large, multi-billion-dollar company where we went to two crews and finished the job in nineteen weeks instead of twenty-six. However, up until this point we'd stuck with things I knew how to do. I was about to learn that I was afraid to do any construction projects that I had never done before.

Because of our recent breakthrough with this large public company, my confidence was high. I was beginning to learn what God can do with a supernatural business when we are praying, operating in integrity, living in humility, and seeking to serve others. But God doesn't teach you how to be courageous in a classroom. He began to teach us about courage as we experienced frightening challenges and difficulties in our lives and business. We were committed to doing things His way, and as we stuck with it, He helped us overcome. Whenever you overcome the fear that comes along with problems, it builds confidence and character and faith in God, which will never disappoint (check out Romans 5:3-5).

Crashing Through Roadblocks

God helped build my confidence through a series of jobs that expanded our borders. I heard that a very well-known property holding company had a lot of projects and around twenty million dollars' worth of renovations doing the new kind of work we'd just started. So, I connected with them and arranged a meeting, but they told me they'd already hired a contractor for all six projects. "Thanks for checking in," they told me, "but we already have someone."

That is when I felt like God told me, "These are your jobs." He was about to teach me a powerful lesson for any supernatural business: **Just because there's a roadblock doesn't mean it's not God.**

All too often, we think that if it's God, it will be easy. We want smooth sailing, no interruptions, and for it all to take just one phone call or meeting. When we encounter a roadblock, we can be tempted to doubt and fear. God wants to develop our courage and our character, and we do this best by pushing through frightening and difficult situations, finding the good things He has for us on the other side of our fear.

You do not develop courage when everything is easy; you build courage when you persevere in the face of fear.

You may remember the story I told of contacting the people from this very well-known property holding company repeatedly. Eventually after I'd reached out to them over the course of weeks, I was positioned to help them with a project that started the long-lasting relationship I had with that company.

Because of the confidence I had gained in tackling the big job for the multi-billion-dollar company and had in God, I was able to follow that feeling that these jobs were for me, despite the roadblocks. This is a great example of persevering.

He Is All You Need

God will call us into new territory, personally and in supernatural business, but we must be willing to step out. For me, stepping out in one project meant doing sheet metal work. I'd never done sheet metal work before, but one job with that multi-billion-dollar company meant doing some sheet metal in addition to the carpentry, patio fencing, stucco, and other aspects I was familiar with. They wanted me to do the project, but I was hesitant because they insisted that the metalwork component was part of the job.

I told them, "Listen, I'm sorry. I don't do sheet metal. I've never done it before. I don't understand it, and I'm not comfortable doing something I've never done before."

They said, "Well, the sheet metal is included as part of the scope of work. As the general you must take it all, and if you don't do the sheet metal, then you don't get the rest of the job."

However, I had such a great relationship with that multi-billion-dollar company at that point that the construction manager told me they had a bid from a sheet metal contractor and they'd pay me an extra 10 percent to manage his part of the project. I asked if I could have some time to think it over, and the construction manager told me, "Yeah. You have ten minutes."

I stepped outside to think. I can still remember it like yesterday—it was on Irvine Avenue, one of the busiest streets in Newport Beach. The sound of the traffic masked the sound as I cried out to God, "I don't know how to do this. God, I don't know what to do! This is not what I do. How do I start to do something that I don't know how to do? I have no experience in this. This is huge exposure. I've heard of people going out of business for doing stuff they don't know how to do . . . . "

That was when God said something to me that He has said two or three times over my career: "I am all you need."

I was about to learn courage by doing something that frightened me. I asked God, "Okay, what do I do?" I felt like He was telling me to go back in there and sign that contract. So I went back into the construction manager's office, and with my hand literally shaking, I signed that contract.

I went back to the office and called a friend of mine who worked for another company. I knew he understood sheet metal, so I asked if he'd be willing to look over the work detail and give me some pointers on how to make sure it's done right. He said, "Oh, Mike, this is the simplest sheet metal detail that I've ever seen."

I replied, "Okay. Well, it's simple for you. You'd know how to do this. Not to me—I don't know anything about sheet metal."

He asked if I wanted him to send out a couple of bids, and after I looked over the contract and saw that it didn't stipulate I had to use the guy the construction manager had told me about, I said to go ahead. The original contractor's bid was for $73,000, and my friend got me a bid for $64,000—and it was a guy he vouched for personally.

I started walking around my office saying, "I just made $9,000!" In fact, it was the day God took me from being a contractor to being a businessman. Then I realized that they were going to pay me $81,000 to manage the metal work regardless of how much the contractor's bid was!

When I told the original contractor that I was going to give the job to someone with a lower bid, he asked if he could sharpen his pencil and get me a better bid. He told me he wanted the job because his shop was just down the street, and he ended up coming back with a bid that almost made me fall out of my chair: $48,000.

My contract was that they were paying me $81,000 to manage this part of the project because his original bid was $73,000, but now he was going to do it for just $48,000. I was going to make $33,000 extra on a job I had tried hard not to do because I was afraid of the exposure! The contractor did a fabulous job, and because of my friend that had sent out the bids, I was able to learn what to look for with sheet metal work, and MRC expanded into a new area of construction.

My confidence, and sense of business took a huge leap forward. Because of that job, I was able to do others, and I could show them something that demonstrated what MRC was capable of. Without that job with the multi-billion-dollar company and breaking through the fear, I would never have gotten many others. Probably 80 percent of the jobs I have done in the last two decades were directly connected to pushing through that fear and doing that big job.

However, God did not just expand us to prosper MRC: Because we got all of those fantastic jobs, we ended up being able to build several churches! In addition, the money that came in allowed us to send roughly fifteen missionaries out around the world.

All of that would never have happened if I hadn't overcome the fear of doing something I've never done before. Everything you want is on the other side of your fear. God is ready to expand your territory, but it is up to you to step out when He tells you, push through the roadblocks, and learn courage by defying fear.

Water Walker

Sometimes I ask people if fear is a good or a bad thing. Many in Christian circles will say it's a bad one, but I want to make them think, so I ask them to hold on a second. If we learn that something can hurt us the hard way, we learn to not do that thing. That fear can help prevent us from hurting ourselves worse or again. I'm afraid of hurting my wife, and that fear stops me from saying stupid stuff. Over time, I have learned from my mistakes.

But the fear that freezes us and stops us from moving forward is never a good thing. We do not want to be frozen, unable to make decisions and move. That is never productive, especially in business. Healthy fear can protect us, but unhealthy fear will freeze us.

One favorite scripture tells us God has not given you fear that will make you timid and unable to move (check out 2 Timothy 1:7). Instead, God gives you His Spirit—a Spirit of power, a Spirit of love, and the fruit of self-discipline and a sound mind. That sound mind allows you to continue to think creatively, even when afraid.

That is because sometimes you must step forward and do whatever He has told you to do, even when you are scared. So how do we do this? How do we press through and do it even when we are afraid?

The answer is that we must keep our eyes on Jesus. In the Bible, sometimes Peter gets a bad rap. He's the disciple who denied Jesus three times, cut off a guy's ear, and one time was told, "Get behind me, Satan" from Jesus. But the fact is that Peter was the only other man in history to walk on water beside Jesus Himself!

You may have heard the story—Jesus sends the disciples out ahead of Him to cross the lake in the boat, and while they're out there, a fierce storm comes up. They row *all night*. While they're still far away from land, massive waves are crashing over their boat when suddenly they see Jesus *walking* across the surface of the lake!

What's the first thing Jesus tells them? *"'Don't be afraid,'* he said. *'Take courage. I am here!'"* (Matthew 14:27 NLT).

This is why I love Peter: It says, *"Peter, suddenly bold, said, 'Master, if it's really you, call me to come to you on the water.'"* So Jesus answers, *"Come ahead"* (Matthew 14:28-29 MSG).

Peter may have been quick to run his mouth, but he was also ready to take a step of faith that no one else did. He also teaches us the first lesson about learning courage: **When you are going to step out of the boat, you need to be sure it's Jesus who is calling you.**

It is not courage to step out of the boat when it's not Jesus calling you. If you do that, you'll drown. I do not take huge risks unless I'm sure I have actually heard from God and have peace about it. That "peace" is important—to me, it means things such as agreement with my wife. If she is not in agreement about stepping into something I've never done before, I'm not going to do it. This is one reason it's so important to give your spouse the right to speak into your life—

and that you have already agreed in advance that you'll listen. I have found that the voice of God and the voice of my wife sound a lot alike! We will talk more about this in the chapter on honor, but the reason I know agreement is so important in our marriage and the decisions that we make is that I can directly see how the biggest mistakes I've made trace back to times when Janet and I were not in agreement.

It is possible for the wind and waves of the storms of life to be all around you . . . but for God to give you the peace to step into something bold and new. When Peter heard Jesus' voice, he recognized the voice of God. He knew it because he had spent so much time with Jesus. So, when Jesus told him to come, Peter had the peace to do the unthinkable and step out of the boat onto the wind-tossed waves.

The next lesson Peter teaches us is to keep our eyes on Jesus. We read that Peter stepped out of the boat and walked to Jesus, but when he looked down at the waves churning beneath his feet, he lost his nerve and started to sink. Peter was doing the impossible, walking on water, but when he took his eyes off Jesus, he stopped walking and began sinking. When you're stepping out into whatever new thing God is calling you to do, don't look at your circumstances; keep your eyes locked on Jesus.

You may have heard that part of the story taught before, but what we rarely hear is how Jesus responded when Peter lost focus. The moment Peter starts to sink, he calls out to Jesus to save him—*and immediately*, Jesus reaches down and grabs his hand!

Know this: If Jesus has called you out of the boat, even if you lose your focus on Him and start to sink, He will save you. He is just that good!

Courage is stepping out of the boat when you hear God calling you. Courage is keeping your eyes on Him, even when your circumstances are raging all around you. And courage is knowing He will save you even if you encounter roadblocks and it looks like you're going down.

Take Courage

My favorite definition of courage is the ability to disregard fear. It isn't that the fear doesn't exist; it's the ability to move forward even when the concern is trying to paralyze you.

Courage is an action. It's not passive, it's active. Look back up to what Jesus told them in Matthew 14:27: *"Take courage!"*

Courage is not given; it's taken.

This theme is throughout the Bible. Over and over, God tells people not to be afraid. It's the most frequent command in His Word! The opposite of being scared is taking courage, and sometimes God tells us to *be* courageous literally.

In the Book of Joshua, we read of Joshua taking over the leadership from Moses. These were big shoes to fill! Many people are familiar with Joshua 1:9: *"This is my command—be strong and courageous! Do not be afraid or discouraged. For the Lord your God is with you wherever you go"* (NLT). I challenge you to look at that first chapter at each time God tells Joshua to be strong and courageous.

God tells Joshua to be courageous three times. He doesn't say He will give Joshua courage; He tells Joshua to be it. God knew that Joshua would need great strength and courage to take the steps forward that were required of him as the new leader of His people, so He told Joshua to get ready. God gave him the secret—*be* courageous.

Sometimes we have warning and can get ready. Other times, when things are going sideways, we must take courage right in the middle of the storm. We read that when David was greatly distressed because he and his men's home had been sacked, everything they owned was stolen, and their families kidnapped, he *"encouraged himself in the Lord his God"* (1 Samuel 30:6 KJV). This means he took courage. It was not given to him; he had to take it, and the courage he took was in God.

Remember, just because God calls you to step out, it does not mean there will not be roadblocks. You may encounter setbacks. And when you do, you need to be ready to actively take courage.

The Courage of Capacity

When you take courage and step out, God will enlarge your capacity. My wife is often asking, "Where did you get all this capacity?" because I do so many different things. I have grown in capacity because I have followed the voice of God when He told me to do something, even when it scared me.

Early on with my company, I was pretty inefficient. I would get a job, start it, complete it, and then look for another. There would be a gap during the time I was looking for the next job. So as God started expanding my capacity, He knew He needed to push me out of my comfort zone.

It started in earnest when a company called me to come to give them a quote. At that time, an average job for me was about $500, and a big job might be $1,000. When I looked at the project, I saw it was going to be about $1,000, so I gave the construction manager a bid. But before he told me whether or not they accepted my proposal, he wanted me to provide him with another quote. "But I just bid this one, and you haven't given it to me yet!" I told him.

He said we'd talk about it later, and he had me look at another one. This one was much bigger—$2,000. I was in drywall heaven! I gave him my bid on that one, and I asked if he was going to provide me with one of the jobs. Instead of answering, he told me he wanted me to go out and look at a third site. It was the biggest drywall repair job I'd ever seen. This one was $3,000!

I didn't think I'd get the biggest one, but I hoped to at least get the second biggest, and I was praying that I'd get at least one of them. So, I called up the construction manager and asked if he'd sign me up on one of those projects because I really needed the work and could start right away.

He told me, "Oh no, we're not going to give you one of the jobs."

What a waste of my time, I thought.

Then he added, "We'd like to give you all three."

I was stunned. I'd never done more than one job before. I was too embarrassed to tell him I couldn't do them, and I asked if I could call him back. As soon as I hung up, I prayed, "God, what do I do?"

This was the first time I heard God tell me, "I'm all you need."

This was $6,000 worth of work when we really needed it. A bit of backstory is that my wife and I had accidentally *both* double tithed three weeks in a row! And since we didn't want to call our pastor and ask for a refund, we were just trusting God that He would come through.

This was the first year my income doubled, and this was how it happened. God expanded my capacity, and where once I had worked one job at a time, I found myself with three different jobs. It was the first time I did more than one, but it wasn't the last—from that point on, I started doing multiple jobs. My capacity began to grow, and now MRC has handled as many as twenty-one jobs going at once—and counting.

At that point, I had two or three guys that worked with me, and in order to do all three, I had to step out and hire a few more. I'd get one site started, and then I'd move to the next and have a couple of guys get that one started. By that point, the first one was wrapping up, and I helped them get the third one going. I remember that it wasn't challenging to do all three after all. It wasn't much different than what I had been doing when I was just doing one job at a time; there was just no time in between. It was more efficient. I discovered the most significant difficulty had been merely in my mind before we got started.

That is the nature of being afraid—**most fear is only in your mind.** Most of the things we fear never happen, and the fear of them itself can keep us frozen, unable to act, and unable to step forward into the expanded capacity God would like us to develop. Win the battle of your mind, and you will be another step closer to winning the battle with fear.

Resist Fear, Draw Close to Hear God

When we're afraid, we don't step out because we are worried we may fail. We make all kinds of excuses, and we will talk ourselves out of following God. In fact, if you show me a person who makes excuses, I will show you a person who is afraid.

When people are afraid, they also resort to blaming someone or something else. They're indecisive. They procrastinate. People locked up by fear will know they're supposed to do something, but they won't step out because they've let the fear control their actions.

Maybe you're supposed to start a business, launch a new product, or give something. If you come up with a list of a hundred excuses or find yourself shifting blame to someone or something else, it's because of fear. If God told you to do it, you need to take courage and step out into what He's told you to do. Remember, when it's God, He's not going to let you drown—though you may encounter some roadblocks.

The people you see and read about who have stepped out were not free of fear. They heard God, overcame their fear by taking courage, and you can do the same. This means that it is imperative to be sure you've heard from God. Many people ask me, "How do you do that?" Let me tell you what God has shown me.

The first thing is that you must start where you are. There's no sense wishing you were somewhere else, and God never gets down on you or holds things against you. If you currently spend little or no time in prayer, begin there guilt-free, and be ready to expand your capacity.

I believe in spending consistent time with God, so make an appointment with Him, and keep it. Consistent time with God is vital to having a supernatural business, so do what you need to do to keep that appointment on your calendar. If you were meeting with a billionaire CEO to be mentored, you would put it on your schedule, and you wouldn't miss that meeting for the world. So why would you treat the King of the Universe any differently?

Set an achievable goal for your time with God, and then do that successfully. The fantastic thing about spending time with Jesus is that the more you do it, the more you want to do it. I greatly desire the wisdom, peace, and understanding He gives me, and I wouldn't trade them for time doing anything else. You'll get there—just keep at it. Gradually expand the time you spend in prayer, stay consistent, and keep that appointment with Him.

God says, *"Call to me and I will answer you and tell you great and unsearchable things you do not know"* (Jeremiah 33:3). God flat out promises that if you ask Him, He will answer you. You can ask Him for wisdom, and He will never make fun of you—He will give it to you (check out James 1:5).

Seek Him First, Then Wait

God has taught me many times how important it is to seek Him first. On one job, I was losing money, and eventually, I prayed about it. I asked God why I was losing money, and I felt like He answered, "You stopped asking Me what jobs to take and what jobs not to take. Not every job you get is from Me."

Not every opportunity is right for you. Not every invitation to step out is from God, so it's vital that you learn to distinguish between God impressing something on you and all the other influences in your life. I've left million-dollar jobs on the table and walked away because I didn't have the okay from God. Learn to pray, "God, if this is from

You, make it crystal clear to me." I wouldn't move forward until I'd spent enough time in prayer to tell if it was God or not. If it was Him, I would feel a sense of peace about even difficult decisions or potentially scary choices. However, when it wasn't God, I would notice I didn't have that sense of peace. Ask Him to make His will clear to you—to tell you exactly what to do. He will do it.

This is the ultimate gesture of being God dependent: that you have set your will down to follow His will for your life. To discern His will, you must first spend time with Him. There is no shortcut, and there is no alternative. Yet there is also nothing like it!

To have a supernatural business, you must pray . . . and wait upon the Lord until you hear from Him. I often ask God to close doors that are not from Him. We'll talk about persistence in the next chapter but know for now that if God shuts a door, you want it closed.

After the economy crashed in 2008, I really needed work. There was a strip mall just down the street from my office that I bid on, and it looked like we were going to get the job. But then the owner told me he wanted to go in a different direction, and we didn't get the work we so badly needed.

I've told you many other stories about persistently praying and asking, but this time I didn't hear from God to do that. Nine months or so later, I happened to be in that same strip mall to pick up my dry cleaning. I asked the cleaner when the construction would be done because I knew that it was perhaps six months' worth of work, if that, and here it was nine months later.

When I told the dry cleaner that the owner should've accepted my bid, he told me, "Oh, you should be thrilled you didn't get this job. The job isn't finished because he hasn't paid anybody."

I walked out the door, and immediately felt like the Lord told me, "I protected you from that job."

Real courage isn't always stepping out when God says to. Sometimes it's standing fast when He says no. Are you willing to obey when He shuts the door . . . or is silent? That, too, takes courage.

In my own life, I had to learn to understand that seeing the downside was not the same as being afraid. It's important to separate them; we are supposed to be wise, but we aren't supposed to make decisions out of fear. God started teaching me this with the first Oakwood contract that they gave me. I only saw the upside, and it took an attorney looking it over to tell me to watch out for the downside that contract exposed me to.

Even after some back and forth on the details of the contract, I still wasn't sure, and I prayed about it a lot. My attorney said not to sign it, but I wanted to hear from the Lord. "God," I asked, "is this a job I'm supposed to do?"

God taught me that sometimes contracts aren't as important as everybody thinks. The people you're dealing with can be much more important. If you're dealing with a bad person, it doesn't matter how good your contract is—they can find a way to do you wrong. Though this was a strict contract with Oakwood, according to my attorney, the Oakwood people were the best people in the world.

You're much better off trusting God than any attorney. I felt confident that He was telling me to move forward, so I did so—against the advice of my lawyer. So be willing to step out when He says to, but be prepared to wait if He does not.

God's Word to You

As you learn to hear the voice of God, you will find it very helpful to know what He has said in the past. In fact, God mainly speaks through the Bible, so knowledge of the Bible is essential. I talk a lot about hearing from God in prayer, but the first and foremost way that

He speaks to me is through Scripture. He might bring a verse to my mind, or I'll read something, and it will speak to the question I have.

Many times, I know how to respond to circumstances because I have read about similar ones in the Bible. God will answer a lot of your questions this way, and there may not be a need to speak something unique to you. If you spend a lot of time in His Book, He will transfer His wisdom to you through it!

Something you hear from Him in prayer will *never* contradict Scripture. God will always agree with what it says—*always*. The Bible is the trump card, and everything else must agree with it, so start developing a working knowledge of God's Word as soon as you can. You don't have to be a theologian, but how smart is it to read leadership books but neglect the ultimate "letter" ever written?

God will address many of your fears if you will just let Him. Spend time in prayer, and spend time getting to know the Bible—you will never regret it!

Pray, Then Obey

Stepping out in obedience defeats fear. God taught me this in a big way just as we were starting to make real money. The whole time Janet and I had been married, we had never made more than $100,000 together before 1998. Yet as we were experiencing breakthroughs with MRC, we felt like God spoke to us and said, "If I gave you the opportunity, would you give away $100,000?"

We didn't know what this meant, but we decided that we were willing. I remember looking at how much we'd given in December of 1999 and seeing that we had given $63,000. We'd never given more than $15,000 before, so this was a tremendous amount. Then we remembered what God had said, and we saw that we had exactly $37,000 in our bank account.

I told my pastor about what God had said, and he cautioned us to be sure we'd prayed about it. His wife, however, was more direct. She told us, "I can't tell you what to do. But I will tell you this: If you obey God, your life will never be the same."

I am telling you that right now: **If you will take courage and obey God, your life will change.** It will never be the same, and it will not only improve your life, but it will also change the lives of your family and many others because that's just how God works—His blessings are not only for you!

Despite that word of encouragement from our pastor's wife, I was afraid. I frantically looked through the Word for a scripture that said it is okay for us not to give it this year but next year. Instead, I found 2 Corinthians 8:10-11: "*And here is my judgment about what is best for you in this matter. Last year you were the first not only to give but also to have the desire to do so. Now finish the work, so that your eager willingness to do it may be matched by your completion of it, according to your means.*"

That's pretty direct. So, my wife and I got out our checkbook, and with my hand shaking, I wrote a check for everything we had—$37,000.

If God tells you to step out, don't you dare stay in the boat!

Our lives were never the same. Three months later, the former middle manager at that multi-billion-dollar company took me as a partner to learn to buy and sell real estate, and it was after this that God began to double—and even triple—my business year after year.

Fear will keep you frozen in the boat. Fear will prevent you from experiencing God's best for you. It will keep your capacity small, and it will urge you not to trust your Father. But if you will trust Him—if you will take courage and obey whatever He tells you to do—you will never be the same, and neither will your business.

CHAPTER 8:

The Power of Perseverance

The economic downturn in 2007 didn't affect my business in multi-family dwellings, and I thought we were going to be okay. That is until Lehman Brothers crashed in October of 2008. When that happened, it was a direct connection to the financing and interest rates of real estate, and that instantly impacted our business.

When the crash happened, we were reviewing thirty sets of blueprints to give bids, and of those thirty, we could expect to get contracts on half of them. So, I expected that we had about fifteen jobs lining up, but in one day, twenty of those jobs were outright canceled—the projects killed all at the same time. We now had ten sets of blueprints that were actual potential jobs, and of those ten, only one ended up happening—and we didn't get it.

For a lot of people, it was time to panic. I started making some calls, and the problem wasn't that people weren't taking or returning my calls—it was that their phone numbers were *disconnected*. These weren't small organizations, either; these were big players in the market who owned large multi-family dwellings.

It was during this substantial economic crash that the Lord spoke to me and said, "Now is the time for you to do marketing."

Marketing? I thought. For what? There were no jobs!

When I told my staff about this, they politely said, "We don't think this is a good idea. We think you should maximize whatever we're doing right now and not spend money." We had some liquidity, but it wouldn't last forever. No one thought that we should spend money now on marketing for jobs that just didn't exist.

However, I felt like the Lord had been obvious and that now was the time to start marketing. So, we launched a marketing campaign while the economy crashed. It made no natural sense—but God often doesn't! He makes supernatural sense, and it is always in the best interest of a supernatural business to follow God's knowledge, not the world's.

I quickly learned that our existing clients represented just *3 percent* of our target market. We'd been operating MRC while tapping only that small percentage when there were thirty-three times more clients out there to talk to! We created a database of those potential clients, and we started calling them. None of them had any jobs, but they did take our calls.

Hold Fast

We went one whole year without the marketing campaign resulting in a single job. People in the office were frustrated with me because I was spending our liquidity on a marketing campaign for something that didn't exist—at least in their perspective. We spent $75,000 the first year with no results, and then another six months went by before we got our first job. By now I'd spent over $100,000, and that first job netted $28,000 profit. The executive team was now questioning my leadership, but I maintained that this was what we were supposed to be doing.

Remember, before you step out of the boat, you must make sure it's God. But if you're sure, the only reasonable action on your part is to persevere in whatever He told you to do. I had stepped out, and until God told me to do something else, I wasn't going to let circumstances change my mind. So, we kept marketing.

After twenty months, we signed our second job, and it brought a net profit of $275,000, and suddenly not only had we paid for all the marketing, we had something above that. The very people who'd begun to question my leadership started to admit that maybe it was the right thing to do after all. Three months later, we signed another job that made another couple hundred thousand. And two-and-a-half years after God told me to start a marketing campaign, I signed a job for twenty-five million dollars!

That job led to another one six months later, that was another twenty-five million dollars, which led to *another*, in addition to a bunch of jobs that brought in five and ten million each. We had taken a massive step forward, and it was because God had us persevere in marketing when everything said we should not spend the money. In hindsight, the only thing I'd do differently if I had the chance . . . would be to have spent triple on marketing!

If God told you to do something, you don't stop—you keep doing it until He says stop. You step out, and you keep putting yourself out there until you receive what He has promised for you. The power of perseverance is that those hard times build character and if you hang in there, you will see God's goodness to you.

Paul, who wrote a lot of the last half of the Bible, wrote this: *"We can rejoice, too, when we run into problems and trials, for we know that they help us develop endurance. And endurance develops strength of character, and character strengthens our confident hope of salvation. And this hope will not lead to disappointment . . . "* (Romans 5:3-5a NLT).

At one point, we had jobs lined up for two and a half years—so much work that our departments couldn't handle another job. We didn't even have people to bid on more projects, which frustrated the marketing team. We had more work than we could do, and it would not have happened had we not begun marketing when God told me.

In stocks, the only way to ride out market fluctuations is to stay in it for the long haul. You've got to ride out the low times in the market because if you try to hop in and out, you'll either lose your money or fail to see the returns of those who merely persevere through good times and bad. That's how I felt—I was in too deep to quit doing what God had said to do.

Own It

Humility precedes perseverance because you must be humble enough to hear from and follow God. If you don't, you will persist in the wrong things. I've done that, too.

At one point, I thought it would be a good idea to add to the types of construction work we do, and I hired a guy to take us beyond renovations and into constructing new buildings. I probably spent over $300,000 of company money trying to chase after these new construction jobs, but we found out this wasn't our thing. After fourteen fruitless months, I let the new hire go. He just wasn't a good fit for our company, and neither was that type of work, and it was time for me to own up to that and move on.

At the next manager's meeting, I stood up and owned it. "I tried this," I told them, "and it didn't work. It was my mistake."

It is as important to hear God in the middle of something as it is before you start. I already told you to go when He says go and to persevere until He says stop, but you must also be ready to stop and change direction when He says to. Have the humility to own it and then move on. There's no shame or disapproval on you, so learn from these experiences and move forward. God is always looking forward, and He does not hold your past against you.

Serve with Perseverance

Remember, just because you experience roadblocks, it does not mean that something is not from God. Remember the project where I insisted he come to the job site? That was a great example of that principle. We got the job, but then it got put on hold because they couldn't secure financing. At this time, banks weren't loaning money for anything. Eventually, they told me that the job wasn't even going to happen because they couldn't line up the money.

I asked, "What do we need to make this job happen?"

They said, "We have to get financing, but we have a billion dollars in assets to put up."

"So, if you could get financing, the job will happen?" I asked. They said that was the case, so I told them, "Okay. I'm going to call everybody that I know."

I got on the phone, and eventually, I lined up someone who said that they would do it. The company ended up being inspired by my actions. However, I lined up another lender at a better rate. They were so impressed that I would go the extra mile for them, they happily referred us whenever they got the chance.

The project was bonded, and we found out that the company that was hired to do the mechanical, electrical, and plumbing was in a terrible position economically and couldn't get bonded. Therefore, we had to go further to serve this client—we extended ourselves to bond the other company, against the insurance company's recommendation. However, without them, we weren't qualified to do the work.

When we got about 80 percent through the project, the company we bonded went bankrupt! We'd known they were struggling, so we didn't over-release the money. There was enough to do the project, but my people didn't have the skills to replace the bankrupted company. However, God gave the team and me an idea: We hired the newly released employees from the bankrupted company directly to do the rest of the mechanical, electrical, and plumbing work for us. Better yet, we got to pick and choose from among them to get the outstanding ones.

The trustee in the bankruptcy had a million dollars in retention owed to the creditors, so we arranged that they would get their money when we finished the job since they hadn't finished their part. We agreed to pay $650,000 instead of the million because we took on their warranty.

I ended up finishing the project anyway, getting an additional $350,000, and now had my own mechanical, electrical, and plumbing division. Each step along the way, roadblocks threatened to derail this project. However, God knew what we needed, and because of Him, we knew to persevere in the face of adverse circumstances.

James writes, *"Consider it pure joy, my brothers and sisters, whenever you face trials of many kinds because you know that the testing of your faith produces perseverance. Let perseverance finish its work so that you may be mature and complete, not lacking anything"* (James 1:2-4). Do you know why you can consider it "pure joy"? Because you know that perseverance is creating character. Under pressure, your faith is forced into the open and shows its true colors, and as God refines you, you look more and more like Him.

Perseverance Sets the Stage

The company we bonded and went bankrupt had also given us another bid on the second project that helped keep us afloat during the bad economy—The Dream Center I told you about earlier. We had come in so far under the other bidders at twenty-five million instead of thirty-eight million, but without the bankrupted company, we would not be able to do the work—except, we were able to hire the best of their employees!

We had honored God by doing our very best for Matthew and Tommy Barnett, and though we didn't know it, God had positioned us to go the extra mile for them. Because we persevered on the condo project, we gained the mechanical, electrical, and plumbing personnel to do the work ourselves, which saved The Dream Center at least three million dollars right there. It also kept our guys busy during a lousy economy when other companies were going out of business.

Don't Sweat the Small Stuff

There is no perseverance without difficulty, but it's important to remember that not every little thing is a "trial." A trial is difficulty with a purpose.

However, a lot of the little random things in this life are just gnats. These pesky things are not trials. They're just the noise of life. Remember, if you let everything bother you, you'll always be troubled. If you're easily offended, you will be hurt all the time! Over the years, I've learned to swat gnats when I can, but I have chosen not to sweat the small stuff.

I am still learning to try to avoid creating more problems for myself. One of the most significant ways we do this is in watching what we say. If you watch your self-talk and the words you say to other people, you can save yourself a great deal of difficulty. Sometimes, our troubles are self-inflicted because we don't watch what we say.

When we were looking for our first house, we were working with a realtor for an extended period of time. When we were finally buying our house, she said to me, "Oh my gosh, you've really gained a lot of weight!" Was she correct? Yes, unfortunately, she was. Will I ever work with her again? Probably not. Her words created an unnecessary problem.

You can minimize or avoid a lot of problems by just watching what you say.

You can also minimize or even shorten your trials by being humble. Think of how many problems we have because we want our way instead of accepting God's way! In one of our core scriptures from the chapters on humility, James 4, he tells us that God opposes the proud and gives grace to the humble. Then he writes, *"So humble yourselves before God. Resist the devil, and he will flee from you. Come close to God, and God will come close to you . . . "* (James 4:7-8a NLT).

Not everything is "the devil." But even if it is, the response is the same—humble yourself and draw close to God!

Refine Your "Mettle"

Heat purifies precious metals. When they melt, the smith can draw off the impurities, refining the gold or silver to a purer and more precious form. Though you may not ever enjoy the heat when the trials of this fallen world happen, you can grow to recognize that these difficult times are refining your "mettle"—an old term for your character.

Jesus tells us that in this life we will have troubles but to take courage because He has overcome the world (John 16:33). He has won the war, and the difficulties we experience in this life are the refining fires that develop our character. God does not send these trials, but He definitely uses them for our good. You're not going to escape troubles; they're part of life. However, you can allow the Refiner to purify you as you experience them.

Pass the Test

James writes, *"Blessed is the one who perseveres under trial because, having stood the test, that person will receive the crown of life that the Lord has promised to those who love him"* (James 1:12). When I studied this, I learned that the crown symbolizes a victory, such as by a champion athlete or a general who won a war.

When we face trials and persevere, we have the chance to be victorious. The idea is that when we persist to victory, we pass a test. However, if we try to avoid or sidestep the trial, we can end up taking the same test over and over in different forms.

My daughter Nicole was having trouble with her boss and came to me to talk about it. After listening to what she had to say, I told her that she needed to speak to her boss and discuss the issue. However, she didn't want to do that. She preferred the idea of quitting her job to confronting the trouble. I told her, "You need to deal with it because it's not going to just go away."

I will tell you what I told her: You *can* quit. You *can* avoid the problem. But the same thing you are dealing with now will merely come up again and again until you learn how to pass the test.

In supernatural business, we face many troubles, and perhaps our greatest challenge is learning to handle them God's way. If you face a test and you do not pass, He will allow you to try the test again and again—until you pass it. It is actually because of God's mercy that He allows us many chances to pass our tests and receive the benefits of the growth and refinement. The good news is that once you've passed a test, it becomes easier to pass that same test again later in life.

Often, learning the lesson from a small trial now allows you to pass the more significant tests later. Passing the tests prepares us for future victories, and some of my greatest opportunities have come wrapped in the most significant trials.

Trials are going to happen. The question is: How will you handle them? You cannot control most of them. All you can control is you—your attitude and how you handle the situation. God will help you develop the "mettle" of your character, and He will work everything—even trials—together for your good. Trials are not bad; they are necessary. So, will you have a good attitude and grow in the middle of your difficulty? Or will you feel sorry for yourself and miss the point?

We receive God's promises by having faith and being patient. In fact, in the Greek used in the Bible, patience and perseverance mean the same thing. So, will you be patient, knowing that your perseverance develops the mettle of your character? Will you focus on your troubles? Or will you focus on God and the good work He is doing? When you put your hope in Him instead of the trial ending, you will never be disappointed.

The most significant opportunities of your life will often come disguised as problems and hard work. Keep God's hopeful future for you in mind and persevere through the troubles of life—you never know what you'll find on the other side.

CHAPTER 9:

Honor in the Marketplace

A good friend of mine, Mike Floyd, had a marketing and advertising company on the East coast. He has chosen to honor his customers in difficult times, and those relationships have sometimes yielded unforeseen results. Years ago, he had a client who got behind on his payments. It's typical in business to pressure or harass people into making their payments when they get behind. That's fair because when people work, they should get paid. But Mike always took the perspective that if clients get behind, he works with them and tries to help them.

This one particular client just could not make his payment. Mike just really felt like he should give him a pass. Honestly, in my career I've done that sometimes (but not all the time—just when I felt God leading me to do so). So this particular time my friend Mike said he was going to give this customer a break.

Just a few years later, Mike got the biggest opportunity that he had ever gotten. It was a national company that would create hundreds and hundreds of jobs for him. While he was doing the estimate for this new customer, he asked, "Who referred you to me?" It turns out, the new client was actually referred by the client he worked with several years earlier who couldn't make his payment and Mike had forgiven. He ended up getting this new project, which was hundreds and hundreds of times more value than the amount he left on the table when his client couldn't make his payment, in large part because Mike had chosen not to burn that bridge. He had honored his customer, and now the honor from that relationship was opening a door for him that dishonor never would.

Honor is incredibly powerful because true honor is very rare. You may be familiar with honor in the "honor your parents" context, but what does it mean to honor in a supernatural business?

Paul gives us the key in Romans 12:10 when he tells us, *"Be devoted to one another in love. Honor one another above yourselves."* This is the core of honor—putting others ahead of yourself not just in humility but by giving preference to one another. You may be able to see how the topics we've covered like humility and serving, in particular, make honor possible. Without these values at work in your life, you will not have the foundation for honoring one another.

Honor is vital to the supernatural business because honor opens the door to the supernatural.

I'll try to paint you a picture from my own life. You'll remember that early on I told you to give permission, in advance, to a select few people who can speak into your life—people you have pre-decided you'll listen to. This is a form of honor. You may not want to listen, but you have decided you will respect what they have to say . . . even when it makes you uncomfortable.

For me, one of those people I'd pre-agreed to listen to was my pastor. Around 2004 or 2005, I began to feel a call to minister on a greater scale than one-on-one within my business and with my clients. I wanted to do what I ended up calling ministry in the marketplace, but this ministry could have failed to be born God's way.

My friend and personal coach, Tim Redmond, confirmed to me that I was effective in the ministry I was doing. Tim has coached me through many challenging times, and he is one of the chief people I have asked to speak into my life. I can't tell you how valuable a godly coach is—someone who will ask the tough questions and remind you who you are becoming. Tim has helped prevent me from making many bad decisions and has given me needed perspective. Now he was telling me that I was ready for this next step, and I wanted to do more in ministry.

Specifically, I wanted to do a marketplace prayer group. At the time, I was ushering for my first church as well as serving on the board. The first time I approached my pastor and told him that I felt God calling me to do a marketplace prayer meeting as a ministry of our church, it was just in passing. I don't think I communicated it very well and I didn't have his focus; he told me that they needed me to stay in my capacity as an usher. I deeply respect him, and, remember, he's one of those who I have pre-decided to listen to and trust, so I figured that the timing may not be right.

A month or two later, I asked again. I said, "I really feel like God's leading me this way," but again I didn't really give my pastor the plan of what I wanted to do and caught him at a busy time. Again, he said, "I just don't know." I had been so eager and excited, and I talked to my wife about the conflict I was feeling. I knew God was telling me to do something, but I was not getting the support from this trusted man that I had expected. What was wrong?

My wife's counsel was wise and godly: "Just ask him one more time." This time, I wrote out the whole plan God had given me and explained exactly what I felt He was calling me to do—to get leaders together to pray for our businesses and those of others. I presented it to my pastor when he had the time to focus on what I was trying to communicate.

This time he said yes! Accepting those "no's" required me to put the principles God had been teaching me to work—integrity, humility, serving, courage, and perseverance. The end result was honor. Though I didn't understand, I had chosen to honor my pastor, even when it meant trusting that God's plan for my life included honoring those in authority over me when they said "no." That honor then led to the next step when it was time, and we launched the ministry in the marketplace that God had been inspiring in me.

Ministry in the Marketplace

In 2005, Janet and I began organizing our first event to bring pastors and businesspeople together to pray for a ministry in the marketplace event God had put on my heart. For about six months, I worked my regular job, and I spent about another twenty hours a week promoting the event. We fasted and prayed for the people who would come, and a leadership team met every week to pray for our city and area.

We held the event in the Ronald Reagan Presidential Library, which is a fantastic venue, and 350 business leaders from around the area came! Our first event, people came from all over. We had a great multi-church response. We had someone at lunch time give an altar call in a very not-churchy way, and fifteen people were born again. This was a really big event for us, and God showed me that His hand was on it and it was powerful. People's lives were changed; people were talking about it for months afterwards. It really did something to the atmosphere in our whole region.

After six months pushing hard in preparation for the event and then the event itself, as well as my ordinarily demanding schedule, my wife and I were exhausted. We planned to fly out to the Caribbean to relax the day after the event, which was held on a Saturday. We had invited our pastors to dinner at our house the week before the event to see if they had any insight. They saw the future leadership God was preparing us for, and they knew that with increasing authority comes new responsibility. They knew that if we went ahead with our travel plans—which meant that we wouldn't be in church the Sunday following the event—we could miss out on opportunities and even send the wrong message. Again, this man that I respect and am called to honor was telling me something I frankly didn't want to hear.

To us, it looked like well-earned rest, but our pastors at the time saw that it wasn't the best choice. We had a decision to make. Would we listen to their counsel and honor them, or would we do what we wanted to do?

Janet and I talked about it and prayed together, and we decided to do what they asked and postpone our departure. We changed flights, which cost us hundreds of dollars, and instead of flying directly we ended up having to change planes in Mexico City. In the end, the change cost us a whole day of our vacation time, but we felt that honoring them was the right thing to do.

Not only was the event successful, several people who weren't Christians ended up coming to our church the day after the event, and we were there to greet them!

God doesn't bless that which goes against His principles. It isn't about building our kingdoms—it's about building His. Ministry for us is definitely not about money. Ministry is always about people and lives being changed and connected with God. But ministry is also about the principles we have been talking about, and many of them culminate in this concept of honor—honoring God in reverent fear and honoring one another above ourselves.

Honor in Changing Circumstances

In 2010 my wife asked if we could go to a different church to hear a guest speaker she wanted to hear. We didn't know it yet, but a change was in the air.

My initial impression was not to go, because after all, we were a part of our church. My words may have been something like, "No, I go to *my* church. I don't go to other people's churches." But that was "religion" talking. Being in relationship means listening to God (as I mentioned, for me, can often sound like the voice of my wife!).

"Oh, Mike," Janet said, "please?" Right then, I felt like God was urging me to go with her. So in this moment of great unity, we decided to go to our church first and then to go over and catch the special guest speaker.

When we got to our church, it seemed to me that the music was especially beautiful that day. I could strongly feel the presence of God—stronger than usual. I could never dream of leaving!

However, as we enjoyed God's presence, I felt like I heard Him say, "Your season here is up." I had told many people I would never leave, but here in a single moment, God was telling me differently.

I didn't say anything to Janet. We just sat there side by side, and I was thinking on what God had just said but didn't breathe a word of it to her or anyone else. We went to hear the special guest, but the entire time I was meditating on what God had said.

Three weeks later, Janet and I were sitting in our living room and talking when I told her, "Honey, about three weeks ago, at church I felt like God said our season at our church is up."

She looked over at me sharply. "What?" I thought maybe she didn't believe me, but then she said, "Three weeks ago when I was praying, God told me that our season at our first church was up, and I told Him that if that were true, He'd have to tell you!"

I was surprised—but not shocked. God works in unity, and Janet and I have practiced giving honor to one another above ourselves, so it was His style to speak to us in harmony like this.

However, we didn't know what we were supposed to do next. This was not our idea; it was God telling us that our season there was over. He hadn't yet told us where to go. Remember, this is the church where God had blessed us. We'd helped them renovate, remodel, and even build. God had supernaturally blessed our business while we'd been there, as well as teaching us and causing us to grow under our pastor's leadership. He was a close friend, and I had submitted myself to him and his spiritual authority. I did not want to hurt him or his wife in any way. I knew that when people leave churches, it hurts pastors. I wanted to obey God, but I wanted to continue to honor my pastor. How were we supposed to do that if following God meant leaving his church?

Most of the time when someone leaves a church, there is no relationship afterward—it's like a breakup. You say you'll be friends, but the reality is often that you have nothing to do with one another afterward. We didn't want that.

We ended up deciding to honor them by talking to our pastor and his wife—a very uncomfortable conversation. (Remember when I told you that having a supernatural business meant having difficult conversations? This is an example.) We scheduled a meeting with them, and we said, "We feel like our season here is up. We're not upset with anything. We love you both and the church."

We still give there today as God told us, "I want you to be a blessing and give to this church for the rest of your lives." We also are cautious about honoring them with what we say and do.

I now say that I have two pastors: my first pastor, and the pastor of our current church. I continue to have a strong relationship with our first pastor because our main concern was honoring God and honoring him, even in that transition. Because of that, we were able to hold onto that relationship—though the season changed.

Janet and our first pastor's wife are close; honoring one another made it possible to stay connected. We've been able to help the church in the years since and come alongside to partner with them in multiple situations. That said, I don't think we could have preserved this relationship without honor.

Honor in Relationships

A beautiful Psalm says that harmony is like the sacred oil that was poured over Aaron, Moses' brother (see Psalm 133:2). They used olive oil medicinally in the Bible, but it could also be used to mark things of significance. The idea is that they would've poured this expensive oil on his head, and it would've flowed all over him as a mark of God's favor on him. This is a word picture of doing something extravagant to show this person is special.

Think of how today, modern oil lubricates moving parts so there is less friction and pieces can connect and run smoothly. Honor is that lubricant in relationships. When we honor one another above ourselves—when we humble ourselves to serve others, thinking of them before we think of ourselves—we create an environment of honor.

In a supernatural business, this should begin at the top with you, because that is our model from God. God shows Himself to people in three distinct ways: God the Father, God the Son, and God the Holy Spirit. They are three aspects of the same God, and the way these dynamics all interact demonstrates harmony for us. Jesus didn't consider equality with God something to be grasped; He humbled Himself to honor the Father. He spoke only what the Father told Him, as does the Holy Spirit today. They embody the concept of honor to each other, and this is the model for our relationships.

Ephesians tells us to imitate God in everything we do and to give preference to one another out of respect for Jesus (see Ephesians 5:1,21). This looks different from relationship to relationship and in different seasons, but the common denominator is honor. When we honor God and one another first, it makes everything else work smoothly. When we are selfish and full of pride, it's like sand in the gears between us.

Just as honoring each other on a daily basis helps my marriage with Janet, honor helped the transition of my relationship with my first pastor. For eighteen years, I had a very close relationship with him and called him nearly every day. As our relationship changed, I would sometimes go weeks without talking to him, but I still honored him.

At one point, he told me that he wanted to share something with me but that he knew he was no longer my pastor. I said to him, "Listen, you'll *always* be my pastor." I needed to give him permission again to continue to speak into my life, even though our relationship had changed. I wanted and needed him to continue to feel like he could talk honestly into my life, and he still does.

Ideally, relationships can change. Honor helps lubricate the change and keeps our relationships flexible enough to give and flex instead of breaking under the strain.

Honor Brings the Supernatural

Honor creates an environment where the supernatural can happen. You may remember a story from Jesus' ministry where He went to His hometown, but because of their unbelief, He was unable to do great miracles there. There is a connection between honor and the supernatural. In a place where there is much honor, you will see many miracles. Where there is a lack of honor, you will see a lack of the supernatural.

This starts with honoring God. We honor God by honoring people—and not just people in authority, because while we should absolutely honor people in authority, we should honor all people. We honor God when we treat people with dignity and respect, even when they have absolutely no way to benefit us. Treating people with respect who are in authority over you honors God, but when we treat people who are in a lower position than us with respect and treat them fairly, then that honors God.

We can create an environment of honor in our lives and businesses that welcomes God. I believe it is vital to honor anyone in authority over you. That may mean your boss, obviously includes your parents, and in church, it means your pastor or other spiritual authority. At our new church, some of the executive pastors are younger than I am but are over certain areas, like ministry in the marketplace—which means they're over me. Spiritually, they're a boss to me, and I think it's essential that we honor those people.

I believe in being in close relationship with your pastor. That may not look like having coffee with your senior pastor, depending on the size of your church; perhaps your most direct connection is with an associate pastor or a small group leader. The point is that our part is to honor, and honor operates in relationship.

I gave my former church a copy of my schedule so they'd know what services I would or would not be in town for as a way of honoring them, and I do that for our current church as well. I've been doing it for many years, and they find it very respectful. It also lets them know how they can pray for me, and there's something in placing myself beneath their authority that feels good to do. At MRC, I am the boss, but I'm not the boss in the Kingdom of God, and submitting my schedule reminds me of that fact.

We're to pray for those in authority over us—including political leaders. Instead of tearing them down with our words, what would happen if we prayed for them and honored them, regardless of whether or not we agree with their policies?

You may have heard that before, but at MRC we decided to take it the other direction as well. What would happen if we started speaking only respectfully about our clients? We decided that as a company, we're no longer going to complain internally about our clients. We've been doing that about a year as of this writing, and it has changed the atmosphere to speak well of people, even when we may be frustrated with them. If something isn't working, we talk to them—we don't complain about them behind their backs. We honor people with how we speak about them, and how we talk about them shapes the environment.

When it comes to time, how we use our time and respecting other people's time shows honor. I try to honor other people's time by doing things like coming prepared to meetings and emailing or texting to request a call. Well, at MRC we also have a policy that everyone checks in with the receptionist. A guy also named Mike on our team at MRC just walked into my office one day without an appointment. I was in the middle of something, and I said, "Hi, Mike. Hey, can you close the door—with you on the other side of it?"

"What's the problem?" he asked.

"Well, you didn't tell me you're coming—you just walked in here without even telling the receptionist." He had disregarded her job of helping manage the office traffic. She was aware of who was available and what they were working on, including if they were working on something really important. Unless the building was burning down, I wanted him to give me the respect of at least telling me he's coming. I had something important to do, and he was interrupting—friend or not. We show people how much we honor and respect them by how we treat their time; we do not assume that our priorities are more important than whatever it is they're doing.

Honor Produces Unity

Earlier I mentioned that honor was the lubricant that eases relationships. The Psalm I mentioned begins like this: "*How good and pleasant it is when God's people live together in unity!*" (Psalm 133:1). This kind of harmony is what happens when we honor one another, and it creates something amazing—an atmosphere of *agreement*.

In Philippians, Paul writes that if we've gotten anything at all out of following Jesus, if His love has made any difference in our lives, if being in a community of the Spirit means anything to us, and if we have a heart and care we should be in agreement with each other and love each other. Honor produces this agreement. He says, "*Put yourself aside, and help others get ahead. Don't be obsessed with getting your own advantage. Forget yourselves long enough to lend a helping hand*" (Philippians 2:3-4 MSG). In other words, honor one another more than yourselves.

I want to be in agreement with my pastors and church, and my honoring them helps create unity. But believe me, the closer the relationship, the more powerful and fantastic harmony becomes. If you've never experienced it, let me tell you that true harmony and agreement with your spouse is *fantastic*. I've made some big mistakes—hundreds of thousands of dollars—and I can directly trace the biggest mistakes I've ever made to the times where we were not in unity, but I moved ahead anyway.

Agreement will entirely change the dynamic of your home. Instead of just tolerating each other, honoring each other before yourself will produce unity and harmony and improve your family's atmosphere. When Janet and I have been in agreement that God was telling us to do something, it has *always* worked out in our business—every single thing. It is *powerful*!

Believe it or not, unity can change the climate at a supernatural business as well. Imagine working like a well-oiled unit in harmony and agreement. How would that affect teamwork, collaboration, and interactions—both within your business and without? A culture of honor has remade the atmosphere of MRC, and it leaves its mark on every job. Honor makes the situation win-win, and it raises our ability to serve our clients to a whole other level.

No, our company isn't one worship or prayer meeting after another—we're working. We speak the truth in love and don't all quote Bible verses to each other. We work in unity and harmony and get far more done than we'd accomplish without the atmosphere of honor. You can feel the difference in our office, and I guarantee that our clients can feel it as well. Imagine what could change when you promote honor in your supernatural business!

When we, at MRC, are in this state of unity and agreement, it looks like people working together for a common goal and purpose. It's really part of our company culture to be in unity. How do we do that? We do things such as consistently communicating the goals and the vision of the company so we collaborate together as a team. So when you do that and everyone in leadership gets to voice how they feel about a direction or a project or a goal the company has, it creates a sense of buy-in and a culture of unity. We have found that when we work together in unity, God likes to bless it. This works in business, marriage, church, and family.

Honor on the Battlefield

As I mentioned earlier when we were talking about trials, this life can be a battle! As long as we have troubles, we will need people who will stand with us. Honor can look like supporting friends and loved ones when they're in a battle. When we serve by helping them with their difficulties, we're honoring them.

Clients I've stood with during difficult times are incredibly grateful. When I could have thrown them under the bus but instead chose to honor them, I built trust. When they need help, I'm the first one they call. That kind of honor is not soon forgotten—people remember who stood with them in the dark times. At your church, that may look like standing by those in spiritual authority when they have to make a stand for God's ways in ways that go against popular culture.

Honor is like oil. It will reshape your home and your business. It creates the harmony that will turn your business into a supernatural one because it will create the unity that leads to an atmosphere of agreement. Wait and see what God does when you show honor!

CHAPTER 10

Changing the Atmosphere

In the previous chapter, I talked about how honoring one another creates unity and changes the atmosphere, but the power this has to transform a business (even a "Christian" business) into a supernatural one is so important, I want to spend more time here. You will note that we have progressed from the most essential foundations of integrity, to humility, to serving, to courage, and to perseverance before we talked about honor because each has built upon one another. While these are not the only character traits God desires to develop in us, these are the ones God has focused on most in my own life. Together, these characteristics and a selection of others have changed the atmosphere at Mike Rovner Construction from a business, to a Christian business, to a supernatural business.

Every year, I pray and with God's help pick a topic for the year. The year before I wrote this book, it was changing the atmosphere. In our superintendent meeting for that year, this became our theme, and we started implementing things I've told you about such as not complaining about our clients. The increased agreement and harmony that resulted has made us better at collaborating within the company and with our clients, and because we are in unity with them, we have made it our focus to help our clients win.

It is no coincidence that year was the best our company has *ever* had. God began showing me how all of the characteristics we have talked about come together to change the atmosphere, to transform a company into a supernatural business.

Changing the atmosphere at MRC started in our superintendent meeting, and then I preached it at church; I spoke nine different times at nine different churches that year, and God was just ingraining in me the idea of a supernatural atmosphere. I thought that if God could do it at a church, why not at a business?

The honor we showed one another started turning into amazing ideas. We began having raffles on Monday mornings for cool gear like drills, tape measures, or T-shirts. We also started recognizing a team member who really exemplifies the company's core values. Mondays actually became fun, with people coming to work with a positive expectation. Everyone likes being recognized for doing a good job and winning free stuff! But my point isn't to give you a list of the things we did to make things more fun at MRC. Instead, I want you to understand the culture change.

I will tell you this, though: The change in culture didn't end with our office and on our job sites. It included how we handled our clients (no longer talking negatively about them and complaining) and how we decided to work with our vendors and contractors.

Don't Kick People

As we were praying and following God's directions for changing the atmosphere at MRC, I got a call that a job we were doing in Northern California wasn't going well. The owner was complaining that our team was fighting with his team and the subcontractors were fighting with the vendors. Everyone was fighting, and the job was at a standstill.

I eventually got to the bottom of the trouble—a subcontractor was not doing his job because after he bid on the job, his price of materials increased by 40 percent. He didn't want to do his job because he was losing money—he was in a bad place. I decided I was going to go up there to see what I could do to help.

I flew up and met with our team. "Listen," I told them, "this guy is in trouble. He's losing money." They understood that, but they were focused on the fact that they needed him to get his work done. "I understand that, but you can't kick someone when he's down. As a company, we don't kick people, especially when they're down."

"Here's what I want you to do," I told them. "I want you to give him all the extra help you can. If he needs some extra labor, give him a hand. If he needs some materials, give them to him. If he needs nails and we've got nails, give him some nails." I really wanted them to understand something: "If he fails, we fail." I wanted them to treat him as though he worked for MRC—not as a subcontractor, but like an employee. I also put a stop to an email exchange that was totally out of control. I reminded our people that we were only going to speak well of people and not be so negative.

Then I went to meet with the subcontractor. He was angry, and he started venting to me about how he was losing money. He started raising his voice to me, and a part of me wanted to yell back, "Do your job!"

Instead, I said, "I understand." I said that about three times, and each time his voice went down a little bit. Finally, I told him, "I'm up here to help you. My guys are going to help you, and I'm going to talk to the owner and see if he will work with us so you can complete the job."

I got a call the next week from the owner. He asked me, "Did you go to a class on construction efficiency and production?" I told him I hadn't, and he said, "When you left the job, the production picked up by over 40 percent. I don't know how you did it, but it's like everything fell into perfect order."

I told him, "No, I didn't go to a class. I just changed the atmosphere."

It started with us—how we treated that subcontractor, even when we were frustrated with him. We could not control the owner, but we could control our own behavior. I could communicate to that subcontractor that I understood his situation and make him feel heard. And I could intercede on his behalf with the owner, because I knew that if he failed, we'd fail.

I chose to honor him and bring harmony to the situation. As the situation changed and everyone started getting along, it raised productivity.

Change the Atmosphere, Change Lives

When you let God change things, you never know how it will impact someone's life. I was doing the second job for Oakwood, a big company whose business meant a lot to us. I had to work with a wrought iron subcontractor, Gerado, who was very good at doing his work but not so talented at negotiation.

He told me his price for the job was $350,000, and that was quite a bit over the budget. I told him so, and he said, "I really need this job. The lowest I can go is $310,000." I had $325,000 in the budget for the work, and I could tell that doing it for $310,000 was going to be a stretch for him.

I could easily have taken advantage of Gerado and kept the difference, but I knew that wouldn't be good for him. I felt like I needed to change the atmosphere in that relationship, so I blew all my negotiating cards by telling him the budget and that I would give it all to him. Gerado was happy that I hadn't taken him up on the lower amount. He did a great job on the project—he's a true craftsman.

In fact, he did such a good job, we started using him repeatedly. He's probably done thirty or even forty jobs over the course of nearly twenty years for our company, and that first job was simply the beginning of a very good working relationship. The quality of his work is one of the things that has contributed to MRC's good reputation.

But that's not all—God wasn't done.

When we were constructing the building for our previous church, which I mentioned at the beginning of the book, I asked Gerado to come out and give me an estimate. When I got there, he was already installing the wrought iron. I told him, "Hey, you can't just get started without telling me how much first."

He said, "Oh, no. I'm not charging you. I'm doing this work at your church for free. This is your church. I cannot charge for it."

This was a big blessing, but God *still* wasn't done! Gerado was out there the next day when my pastor came out and started talking to him. They didn't tell me about it at the time, but when I went to church Sunday, I looked over, and guess who was sitting in my church? Gerado!

He was there with his wife and two sons that Sunday, and his whole family came to know Jesus! He now leads small groups and is a powerful man of God.

I have not had the time to detail all of the hundreds upon hundreds of people God has put in our path who have accepted Jesus as a direct result of connecting with our team at MRC. Far greater than any profit or expanding influence is that time and again He has set people free, changed lives, and saved souls as a result of the atmosphere changing at my business.

The true fruit of a supernatural business is the lives God changes because of it. The best benefits you will get from a supernatural business are not of this world, they are of God's Kingdom.

Many Christian business leaders are trying to do the right things— they're not sleeping with their secretary or cheating their customers, and are paying their proper taxes. But these things are just the basics of decency, and they have nothing to do with expanding the

Kingdom of God. Some will pray when they need something and will give occasionally at church, but there is so much more God wants you to experience.

Do you know where Jesus did most of His miracles? It wasn't in the synagogue (their church). It was in the marketplace. Your business is a miracle waiting to happen—the question is, will you believe God enough to step out into it?

Don't Make It Hard

When I talk to people about having a supernatural business, many seem to think it's complicated. This isn't true—to have a supernatural business, you must only believe for it and respond to God as He makes changes within you. I've tried to relate to you the principles God has taught me, but His work within you will be different and unique.

My wife is a great example of this. Janet is a hair stylist, but back when she was the assistant for four busy hairdressers, she would pray as she drove to work. She'd pray, "God, may my hands be the hands of Jesus on these people as I wash their hair."

It is as simple as that. God will use that. Pray that God would use you today and that He would show you any opportunity to serve Him and His Kingdom. Pray that He would use you as a witness in your workplace and give you passion for Him and His Kingdom.

You likely spend at least eight hours a day working—sometimes many more. How will you use those hours to build God's Kingdom instead of your own? Whether you're cutting hair, approving budgets, or signing contracts, you can pray that God will use you to impact people for Him—and He will!

As I was telling a friend about my passion for using our resources for good, he told me, "Mike, God's plan for your life is to be an ambassador for Jesus Christ in your sphere of influence." I knew I was supposed to support the church with finances. That really stuck with me—one way I know something is from God—and it helped me realize each and every person reading this is similarly an ambassador for Jesus where you work. Think of what an ambassador does—he brings a little piece of his home country with him wherever he goes. You are to be like that: a representative of God's Kingdom here on earth.

Jesus made us all His ambassadors when He told His twelve closest friends to share what they'd learned from Him with everyone they met, near and far. Then He promised His Spirit would never leave us (see Matthew 28:19-20). You are not in this alone. You have God's Holy Spirit inside you to help you share what God has done in your life and business (see Acts 1:8). He will give you the passion and enthusiasm to share what God is doing inside of you, because people can feel it when you're really excited about something. If that something is your relationship with God, you will want to share it, and they'll want to hear about it.

That doesn't mean you need to be weird and churchy. Your words can be solid and sane, and when people see that you're not weird or misguided, they may eventually come around (see Titus 2:7-8 MSG).

Think about it like this: When you discover a new song, a way to save money, or an amazing new restaurant, do you feel bad for talking to people about it? No! You want to share, because you're excited. This is the nature of your witness for God. All you need to get started is your story. You don't need to memorize the whole Bible; you just need to tell people what God has done for you. Let Him do the rest.

James tells us that our prayers are powerful and effective, so start by praying for the people you work with. Just be nice to them! Do good things for them—not because you're trying to manipulate but because you genuinely want good things for them. When we do good by people, it silences our critics. Generosity speaks very loudly—often even more loudly than preaching. As I said earlier in the book, they are watching. When other people see you handle your troubles in a way that's consistent with your values, they take notice.

God has sent you out as His ambassador, and your supernatural business can be the vehicle He uses to bring others across your path.

Financial Breakthrough

Breakthrough, including financial breakthrough, is a natural by-product of operating in the supernatural. My wife Janet and I have experienced tremendous financial breakthrough since we decided to allow God to transform our business from a natural one into a supernatural one. I've told you about our business doubling, tripling, then growing more, as well as about giving more in one year than we'd made in entire years before.

God's kind of financial success is totally different than the world's. In the world, people become successful, and it can ruin them because they don't have the character to sustain it. However, when you have let God remake you into a supernatural businessperson, He is making you into the kind of person He can trust with prosperity. Proverbs 10:22 tells us, "*The blessing of the Lord makes a person rich, and he adds no sorrow with it*" (NLT).

The blessings of the Lord empower you to prosper, and it is the kind of lasting success that blesses many others and even future generations. Just look at the history of His people—God has prospered them greatly. The patriarchs of the Old Testament were blessed men, and they in turn blessed a nation and then the world.

Today, the Jewish population is in a very unique position. In the United States, they represent 2 percent of the population, but they control 50 percent of our country's wealth. This is God's *favor*. They believe that God wants to bless them—and He does!

My question for you is this: Do you believe God wants to bless *you*?

If you are still struggling with your sense of self-worth, if you're hung up on your failures and sins and feeling condemned for how you used to live—a decade ago, a year ago, a day ago—then you are still learning the power of God's unmerited favor and grace. He wants to make it clear and replace that doubt with the confidence that you are His, bought with a price, and you are now made right with God because of Jesus. Every blessing He gave to Jesus, He wants to give to you.

Jesus told us that everything is possible for those who believe, and in that vein the first step to financial breakthrough is believing that God actually *wants* to bless you (see Mark 9:23). It's not enough to just believe God exists; He wants you to also truly believe that He rewards you when you honestly seek Him first, before the stuff (Hebrews 11:6). He wants to give you every spiritual blessing.

Paul writes that he had learned how to live and be content when he had nothing and when he had everything. Because he trusted God to bless him no matter what, he could confidently tell them (and us) that God will take care of *everything* we need because His generosity is far greater than anyone else (see Philippians 4:18-20). No one out-gives God!

There are no limits on God's blessing. In fact, He delights in giving good gifts to His people! His plans for you are to prosper you and give you hope, which sounds like a pretty good deal to me (see Jeremiah 29:11).

So what would happen if you really believed that was true? What would happen if you let God turn you into a supernatural business-person and your company into a supernatural business?

I'll tell you—financial breakthrough like you've never experienced before.

A Day in the Life of a Supernatural Business

Life change comes first. Breakthrough comes as a natural result. You don't have to strive for it or "work" for it in your own strength; you draw close to God, and He does the change within you. However, many people ask me what the day of a supernatural businessman looks like. I am careful as I share this, because my schedule may not look like yours. The point is not the schedule, just like the point isn't just "doing" the behaviors we've been talking about. The point is who God is making you into as He transforms you from the inside out. So I share what a day looks like not so you can copy it but so that it may perhaps inspire you.

When I start my day, I like to start worshipping God right along with my first cup of coffee. The coffee may get my mind going, but the worship is what gets my spirit moving. I have a favorite song I've been playing for many years, Rita Springer's "Holy Spirit Come," and it's almost constantly playing in my home and office.

Before I let the requirements of my day jump on me and drive me, I always take the time to start my day with a prayer of thanksgiving. It doesn't have to be long, but I want to fasten my mind on Him first. I might pray, "Thank You, God. Thank You, God, for who You are." I remind myself who He is—all-powerful, all-knowing, ever-present, eternally good, the unchangeable One, He who is the beginning and the end. I want to remind myself of the characteristics of God, because when you have a very big God, you'll notice you have very small problems.

I am a very, very busy man, but no matter how busy my day is, I like to spend at least thirty minutes like this—just praising and worshipping God, thanking Him for who He is. There is no real formula for it, because I do something different every day. Again, the point isn't the religious repetition; the point is just spending time with Him in relationship.

If you have a spouse or children, you can probably identify with this: I love my children very much, and even as they get older, I like to talk to them every day. I don't do it because I have to. I do it because I love them, and I want to hear their voices! Now I'll call them just to talk—no agenda, nothing I want. I just like speaking with them.

This is what time with God should be like—just spending time together.

After I have spent time with God like this, without fail He gives me some direction every day. He will whisper something to me to say or do. Whatever you do to acknowledge God and spend time with Him, I challenge you to *stop and listen* after. God wants to talk to you like a father just wanting to talk with his children. Don't always hijack your time asking for things or just wanting something from God. Instead, simply spend time in His presence. The rest—all the blessing, all the life change, all the power for witnessing—comes as a natural result of spending time with Him.

Relationship is all about communication. Your relationships will only be as healthy as your level of communication, and it is no different with God.

Also, understand that God is not the author of confusion. It isn't His desire to speak with you cryptically and confusingly. I frequently pray, "God, show me what to do today. Make it so crystal clear that there'd be no way I make a mistake." I do this during my commute a lot. I have a short drive to work, so I don't have time for long, religious prayers, and I know that God can and will speak to me with clarity—if I'll *listen*.

When I get to work, before I fire everything up and get lost in email or meetings, I like to write down whatever is on my heart. It often has to do with work, but it may be something else, like someone I should contact and encourage. God will often put people on my heart to call or encourage. I have many sticky notes with little things God has told me under my computer—things like, "Block out the noise," or, "Now is the time to be completely aboveboard and candid with all." These are things I don't want to forget in the busy press of life and work. Whatever you hear when God speaks to you, I encourage you to *write it down*. Remember, in a contract nothing is real until it's in writing;

so too, when you write down what God speaks, it becomes real to you. Trust me, if you don't write it down, you'll forget it in time.

My biggest piece of advice here is to be intentional, yet led by the Spirit. It is a balance, like so many things in Christianity. I look for what the Spirit wants to tell me, but I also have a spreadsheet with the top twenty relationships in my life because I want to make sure I'm touching those people routinely in some way. Many are clients, but others are employees, vendors, pastors, or others that I'm mentoring. I want to ensure I'm reaching out to them at least once a week.

For me, Tuesdays are special. On Tuesdays, I meet with Chuck Damato, our company chaplain. This may not be someone you have on staff, but if you have a person who will agree with you in prayer, it is a powerful way to invest your time—praying together in agreement. We pray through the company and for the people that we're working for. We pray for them to meet Jesus or to know God better—for their families, their marriages, their kids. We pray that they'll be blessed and healed or anything specific we feel inspired to pray about.

Finally, as I'm giving you examples of what I do, I urge you to find a way to give every day. Find a way to serve. Get your focus off of yourself, and make your life about serving and giving as a way of pushing back against life's tendency to capture our attention and focus it on ourselves. Giving is your best defense, and remember that the heart of humility is being God dependent!

Let Your Ideas Ignite

These are just a few things I do, but I hope that they ignite something in you about living and working supernaturally. Remember, the way you start it sets the atmosphere for your day. When the first thing you do is dive into emails, you are setting yourself up for a day dominated by that kind of thinking. When the first thing you do is dive into God, you are setting the stage for a life-changing super-natural atmosphere.

What kind of atmosphere do you want to be breathing all day? The tyranny of the immediate, or the life-giving breath of God? I choose God! Wisdom for your day, the power to obey God, the heart of the Father, and so much more awaits you in the atmosphere of a supernatural business. However long you've been saved, however close to God you are, He is eager for you to draw nearer to Him.

He doesn't want your business to be moral, ethical, or profitable. He wants it to be *supernatural*. He wants to use it to change lives—starting with your own and spreading out from there to employees, vendors, and even clients.

CHAPTER 11:

Believe

We started this book by talking about the fact that you can pursue smart business practices that *seem* right . . . and yet not genuinely grow, thrive, and excel because you're putting your attention on the wrong things—the things of this world, rather than God's priorities. I've done my best to represent to you what a supernatural business looks like.

God's transformation isn't about self-improvement, acquiring new business techniques, or getting Christians to participate in your vision. God wants to change the atmosphere of your life and business and revolutionize how you see yourself, your purpose, and your business. He filled the Bible with stories of people who experienced this kind of life-changing conversion again and again, showing that it was not their hard work, intelligence, or even commitment that made the difference. He did not bless them for being people of integrity, humility, service, courage, or perseverance before He called them.

No, those things were the *result* of God's influence on their lives. They are the outcome of going from a person mired in the natural to one empowered by the supernatural.

I told you early on that I hope this book can shorten your learning curve. My prayer is that you have seen the results of God moving me into the supernatural, and instead of fixating on a character to-do-list, you've seen that it is God who develops these things within you.

So, how do we move forward into this? *Believe.*

Anything Is Possible

I don't know where you are in your journey. It's possible that you are already well along the path where God is developing the supernatural within you and your company. However, it also could be that you have read this book *wanting* to believe. Right now, you may be wishing that these things are real, and you may be thinking that all these stories I've shared are too good to be true.

These stories aren't too good to be true; they're too good not to be God!

There's this great story in the Bible of a man who was burned out, spent, and exhausted. He brought his son to Jesus' disciples so they'd pray for him and heal him, but they were unable to help the boy. So the whole group brings the child to Jesus, and the father asks Jesus to help if He could.

Jesus told this man that anything was possible if a person believes (see Mark 9:22b-23).

Then the father said something that's very encouraging for anyone who is too worn out and tried to conjure up any fake enthusiasm. He cried out that he believed—and then asked Jesus to help him *overcome his unbelief.*

That was all Jesus needed. He prayed for the man's son, and the boy was set free and healed that very moment—permanently.

Permanent transformation is just waiting for you to believe. You may be like that dad right now—burned out and exhausted. Perhaps all you can come up with is telling Jesus you *want* to believe. That's enough for Him to work with.

God wants to change your atmosphere. He wants to change your business's atmosphere. He wants to use you, and it, to make an impact in people's lives.

Will you let Him?

He isn't waiting for your hard work or commitment to forcing your way forward. He wants your belief that He and His ways are more powerful and pertinent to your life and business than anything the world could ever offer.

If that's you—if you believe that you're ready to step out into the supernatural—then it is time to do precisely that. It's time to get out of the boat, despite the wind and waves. It's time to do the right thing, even if it looks like you'll lose money. It's time to do it God's way, even when every business book on the shelf tells you to do the opposite.

If you're ready for a supernatural business, tell God, and step out today into the future He has designed just for you. You will never look back.

Power of Prayer

I want to reiterate this one more time: A supernatural business relies on prayer. If you take nothing else away from this book, go away knowing that a strong personal relationship with God through prayer is the most vital component of your supernatural business.

There is no substitute for you praying for your business, but Christianity was never meant to be lived out alone. We are people of relationships, and a support network of prayer is absolutely essential in my mind. The effective prayers of righteous people have a significant impact, so find people who are committed to prayer and understand prayer's power to change things—and then get them to pray for you and your company! No one can ever tell me prayer doesn't work; I've seen it change people, circumstances, and myself too many times to count. I am utterly and entirely convinced that God answers prayers and performs miracles—I've seen them too many times to think otherwise.

The best decisions I have ever made came after spending time with Jesus. He made me look smart, and He wants to do the same for you! He wants your choices and decisions to look like His and to be empowered by the wisdom only God can give you.

Live with Integrity

If God has given me a life message, it is to live with integrity. A supernatural life and business starts with integrity because it is the foundation God begins with as He transforms our character. Moving from the natural to the supernatural doesn't happen overnight; it is the result of the transformative work of God, and He begins with your character.

As God began to work on my integrity, He began to give me more responsibility and authority. God will promote you as you have the character to sustain it. He doesn't want success to be your undoing, so He ensures that you have a solid foundation of integrity before He begins to promote you. He wove integrity into everything I do and impressed on me that it is one of the most critical parts of the life change He wants to do within every supernatural businessperson.

Your integrity is how you behave when you don't think anyone is watching, but I have learned that someone is *always* watching your example. They are waiting to see how you'll handle challenges, opportunities, and even victories. How will you use the influence this gives you? Will you flirt with the line between what's ethical and unethical? They will watch you try to straddle the fence . . . and if you do, they will watch you fall on the wrong side.

God showed me that the best way to avoid falling on the wrong side of the fence was to stay far, far away from it, and that is what I'm advising to you. Don't see how close you can get without messing up. Embrace integrity and build trust instead. Trust is currency; it can take a lifetime to build but be lost in an instant. Preserve it and protect it with integrity. Allow those within your trusted inner circle the right to hold you to a life of integrity.

Embrace a Lifestyle of Humility

Allowing chosen people to speak into your life requires you to pursue a lifestyle of humility. To help keep me accountable to the integrity God has called me to, I have given certain people permission to speak into my life—and committed, in advance, to listening to them. My wife Janet is first on this list, but I have submitted to my pastors and others as well. This is giving preference to one another, but it is only one part of being humble.

To me, the most significant part of being humble is how it relates to God. The world teaches us to be independent and to rely on ourselves. But God wants us to depend on Him and not our own understanding or ability. When we are entirely God dependent, we are living the reality that it is all about God, not us.

Jesus is our model for this. He is God, yet He humbled Himself to be born in a stable, submitted His will to the Father, and died a humiliating death on the cross. He did all that for us—not out of weakness, but out of strength. He was strength under complete control.

God desires that we live humbly—putting others ahead of ourselves. We're not as doormats but as examples of Jesus to them. This allows us to serve them supernaturally.

Serve Wholeheartedly

Serving others as though we were serving God doesn't happen without God-dependent humility within us. But when we are entirely reliant on Him in humility, it allows us to serve others supernaturally. A business that moves from natural to supernatural will serve their sphere of influence the same way because we are not to be focused on doing it our way—we're focused on living and serving, God's way.

Too many people have tried to serve sacrificially out of their own resources. It doesn't last. They burn out, give themselves dry, and cannot complete God's work for their lives because they were reliant on what they had to offer—and they gave it all away. That is why God has us serve as though we're serving Him, because when it is as unto Him, He provides the resources from His never-ending supply.

God showed me that my actual job is to serve the people I work with and position them to succeed. True service is transformational; I went from just organizing construction projects to understanding that I succeed as I help those I serve to succeed. When we act as the conduit through which God's power flows, we are blessed along the way. It's a natural benefit of serving as Jesus did.

Be Courageous

When we serve out of God's supply, we can trust Him even when things are scary. It might seem frightening to give or serve when you don't have enough for yourself, but courage isn't the absence of fear. Courage is doing the right thing, even when you're afraid.

Fear makes you want to pull back. It makes you want to hold tightly to what you have—your ability and understanding—and to withhold when God has told you to serve and give. Courage inspires you to step out of the boat onto the wind-whipped water next to Jesus . . . and into His design for your future. You may not be able to see where He is taking you, but as long as you keep your eyes on Jesus and not your circumstances, you will have the courage to live and work supernaturally.

Persevere Through Difficulties

We develop courage when we persevere through difficulties in the face of fear. Sometimes, even when it's God, we face roadblocks, and we must show perseverance. It may not come easy even if it's God's will. Are you willing to pray and keep on praying, to work and keep on working, and to believe and keep on believing?

Jesus tells us this kind of perseverance is rewarded. He tells us to knock and keep on knocking and to ask and keep on asking. Sometimes we must hold fast to whatever He has shown us. But how can you be sure of what that is unless you have developed a relationship with Him through prayer? You can't, and this again is why it is so important to spend time with Jesus.

When you're sure it's God, it is your part to step out of the boat, but it is His to provide the next step for your foot. Even when it isn't easy, we are to persevere until He tells us to stop. Perseverance has the power to convert those hard times into character. Every time you press through into God's promises, you are building your trust in Him and courage for the next time. Your capacity grows until you are ready to be a part of God transforming your life and work into something that's bigger than this world—something supernatural.

Honor Produces Miracles

Jesus showed us that honor is the key that unlocks God's miracle-working power. It produces the unity and agreement that oils relationships and the inner workings of your office. When we put ourselves and our advantage aside to honor others, we are demonstrating to God that we put His way first.

The agreement that comes from honor will completely transform the dynamic of your home and your marriage. There is nothing like working in complete unity with your spouse, and that same dynamic can be true in your office as well. I have never regretted waiting to come into agreement with Janet, but many times I have made mistakes when I moved forward without her. Now, imagine that same unity in your office. What if you had that with your other decision makers? What could you accomplish in unity? I bet you could change the culture of your company and transform the atmosphere!

Change the Atmosphere

All of this—all the changes to our character and inner lives—is designed for one purpose: to change the atmosphere of our lives and businesses in a way that shows God's goodness and draws people to Him.

God isn't just interested in you making money. He isn't only interested in you being successful or your business prospering. However, those things will happen when you seek Him and His Kingdom first. When you do it His way and your business becomes a supernatural one, all of the blessings of heaven are the by-product!

Your supernatural business will change the lives of employees, subcontractors, vendors, and even clients. People will come to Jesus, and their lives will be altered forever. God will transform the way they live and work, and this will impact their families. Others will come to God, and the effect will continue to spread. Along the way, God will bless them—and you.

A culture of integrity, humility, service, courage, perseverance, and honor has changed the way we do business at Mike Rovner Construction; but far more importantly, it has transformed hundreds of people's lives. We did not stop working and turn our company into a church. Instead, we brought the supernatural into the marketplace and let it change the way we work on a daily basis.

What does God want to do where you work?

God Wants to Write Your Story

Don't be confused—God doesn't play favorites. If God can do all this through a drug dealer from a broken home like me, He can do it for anyone. He deeply desires to do for you everything He has done for me.

If you want to thrive and excel at life and business, if you want to be an ambassador for God on the job, and if you're going to see a breakthrough, it lies along the path of the supernatural. It is tied to the shift in atmosphere God wants to work within you and your business—to take it from a nice, ethical, even Christian one and transform it into a supernatural one through which He can miraculously change lives.

The change—and the benefits—will start with you, but they are not meant to end with you. The transformation isn't just for your benefit; it is so that you can, in turn, be helpful to others. That's the natural way God works. It is also why God had to lead me into these principles, which I've given you, before He prospered Mike Rovner Construction so much—He knew I'd need to be supernaturally-minded to handle it.

Now, it's your turn. I have done my best to relate to you the things that God taught me through my stories and life lessons. You know the principles, and you've seen examples of them in action throughout this book.

It is now your job to begin to apply them. They will do you no good if they stay head knowledge and do not become heart transformation.

It is my prayer that this book is the catalyst for that change within you and your business. The days of having a natural business are over! The new frontier of a supernatural life is before you.

Your business is a miracle waiting to happen—the question is, will you believe God enough to step out into it? Of course, you will!

Author Contact

If you would like to contact Mike Rovner, find out more information, purchase books, or request him to speak, please contact:

Thrive Teaching
www.thriveteaching.org
info@thriveteaching.org

Mike Rovner Construction, Inc.
5400 Tech Circle
Moorpark, CA 93021
(805) 584-1213
www.rovnerconstruction.com

Follow Mike Rovner
www.facebook.com/MikeRovnerConstruction
www.linkedin.com/company/mike-rovner-construction-inc
www.twitter.com/MikeRovnerInc

About the Author

Mike Rovner is president and founder of Mike Rovner Construction, Inc., ranking among California's most prominent general contractors with 300 employees and $60 million in annual revenues. Together with an exceptional team of industry-recognized professionals, Mike Rovner Construction has completed multi-million-dollar renovation projects for a portfolio of construction industry leaders that includes Shapell Industries, G & K Management Co., Inc., The Irvine Company, Legacy Partners, Essex Property Trust, as well as many others.

Mike Rovner Construction's clients celebrate the company for its steadfast commitment to the highest possible quality workmanship—delivered on time and on budget. That's why Mike Rovner Construction ranks among the top of preferred contractors' lists for prestigious developers and asset management firms throughout California.

Marking more than three decades in the construction industry, Mike Rovner established his company in 1992 following a notable career as a contractor specializing in painting and drywall for residential and multi-family units. His extensive background encompasses estimating, scheduling, and all areas of materials acquisitions and operations, working in tandem with architects, engineers, and designers. In addition, he is noted for his vast experience in working successfully with relevant governmental agencies, bringing to the table longstanding professional relationships that have served to deliver impressive results for client projects.

Faith has always played a pivotal role in Mike Rovner's distinguished professional career—to the degree that he is an in-demand speaker on ethics in business and has authored *Supernatural Business* based on his principles of values and success.

Rovner serves on a variety of non-profit boards and organizations, including the Los Angeles Dream Center, Life Impact International, The City Church Ventura, and he is a member of the Urban Land Institute, Building Industry Association of Southern California (BIASC), California Building Industry Association (CBIA), and the National Association of Home Builders (NAHB).